The  Little League® Guide to Tee Ball

The Little League® Guide to Tee Ball

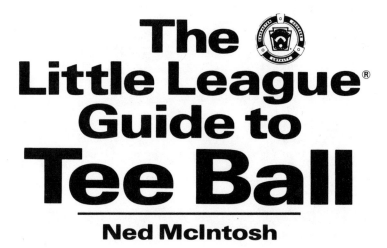

Ned McIntosh

CONTEMPORARY
BOOKS

Library of Congress Cataloging-in-Publication Data

McIntosh, Ned.
    The little league guide to tee ball / Ned McIntosh.
       p.   cm.
    Includes index.
    ISBN 0-8092-3791-1 (pbk.)
    1. T-ball.   I. Title.
GV881.5.M35   1993
796.357′8—dc20   92-45097
                             CIP

3862 1000 165307

Photos by John Krachinski

"Little League Tee Ball for Baseball and Softball" in Chapter 9 reprinted with permission of Little League Baseball, Incorporated.

Little League®, Little League Baseball®, LL®, LLB®, and Little Leaguer® are the principal registered trademarks and service marks of Little League Baseball, Incorporated. These marks are protected both by a special Act of Congress and registrations with the United States Patent and Trademark Office. All rights in and to any and all marks of Little League Baseball, Incorporated, are reserved.

Published by Contemporary Books, Inc.
180 North Michigan Avenue, Chicago, Illinois 60601
Manufactured in the United States of America
International Standard Book Number: 0-8092-3791-1

Dedicated to my grandchildren
and all other boys and girls of the next
generation of Little Leaguers

Contents

Introduction

This is the third book I have written on youth baseball/ softball. All three were published by Contemporary Books, Inc., and all three were approved by Little League, Incorporated, the international organization that sponsors Little League Baseball and Softball.

Managing Little League Baseball was published in 1983, with a foreword by Chuck Tanner, then manager of the Pittsburgh Pirates professional baseball team; *Little League Drills and Strategies* was published four years later. This book on Tee Ball reflects the fact that interest and participation in youth baseball and softball now starts at the much earlier ages of six, seven, and eight for boys and girls rather than the traditional nine-to-twelve age range for Little League Baseball and Softball.

My wife and I are blessed with six children, three boys and three girls. We decided to share parental duties in our children's activities by having me work with the boys in sports, Boy Scouts, and so on, and having her work with the girls in Brownies, Girl Scouts, and so on. You can imagine my surprise when my seven-year-old daughter, Amy, asked me to coach her Tee Ball team, and I had to ask her, "What's Tee Ball?" That was back when Tee Ball was in its infancy in development.

Our first tee was made of a discarded plastic highway cone as the base and a car radiator hose inserted through the top of the cone as the adjustable vertical piece on which you place the ball. (If you have budget problems, you will find this combination very serviceable as a practice tee and a lot less expensive than the commercial tees that are on the market today.)

What caused Tee Ball to become an organized activity, more than anything else, was the overanxious parent who wanted to give his or her child a head start in competitive sports at an earlier—and still earlier—age. I confess to having been one of those overanxious parents who, before Tee Ball, helped organize Minor League Ball as a preparation for Little League. Unfortunately, we found that many seven- and eight-year-old pitchers couldn't even reach the plate, let alone pitch in the strike zone, so we let the coaches pitch. But there was no compensating for the fact that the eye-arm-leg coordination of many seven- and eight-year-olds was not sufficiently developed to hit a pitched ball, no matter who pitched it or how slowly it was pitched. Meanwhile, the defensive players were playing in the infield dirt or picking daisies in the outfield because they were bored. It wasn't much fun!

Then came Tee Ball, which changed all that and became an action-filled, fun game in which everyone— no matter how small or uncoordinated—could hit the ball, run the bases, and score runs; and in which at least two fielders became involved in fielding, throwing, and catching the ball on every play. The enthusiastic squeals of players and parents attest to the fact that it is fun!

The central coaching philosophy of my first two books on Little League was "Keep it simple; make it fun!" Tee Ball is the manifestation of that philosophy: every player bats every inning, every player plays in the field every inning, no one cares about the score, and everybody goes home happy!

Although my first two books received favorable reviews, many of those reviews focused on the chapters dealing with the "bane" of Little League, parental pressure! The headline for the *Chicago Tribune* review of my book *Managing Little League Baseball*, for example, was "Parents Strike Out in New Little League Book."

My fervent hope is that the refreshing "let's let the kids have fun" attitude of Tee Ball, with no parental pressure and no pressure to win, will "percolate" into the higher levels of Little League, particularly for parents.

In organizing this book, I recognize that the parents who read it will include neophytes to Little League—that is, those whose first child is participating in Tee Ball—as well as parents with older children who have participated. Readers will also include parents with a limited amount of time to help their child participate in Tee Ball as well as those who can actively participate by coaching their child and his or her teammates. To speak to all parent readers, the book is organized into three parts: "Starting Out," "Teaching the Basics," and "Keeping a Good Perspective."

PART I
STARTING OUT

1
What Is Little League?

Little League Baseball, Incorporated, is a nonprofit organization founded in 1939 that serves more than 2.7 million children each year throughout the world. It is headquartered in Williamsport, Pennsylvania, where it was started and where the Little League World Series is staged each August. It is truly a "world" series: teams from the U.S., Europe, Canada, Latin America, and the Far East regularly compete for the Little League World Series title, which indicates the worldwide popularity Little League has achieved.

Many major league baseball players started their careers in Little League, and the vast majority of Little League alumni remember the experience as a family rite of passage. Their dads coached, their mothers worked in the refreshment stand, their brothers and sisters came to their games, they made lifelong friends, and who won or lost was forgotten in a sea of pleasant memories.

Little League Baseball, Incorporated, is highly structured, with a distinguished volunteer board of directors and a highly competent professional staff based in Williamsport augmented by regional headquarters staff based in Florida, Texas, California, Indiana, Connecticut, and Canada. Summer camps—two-week sessions—are held in Williamsport and Hillgrove, Pennsylvania, St. Petersburg, Florida, San Bernardino, California, Waco, Texas, and Indianapolis, Indiana.

Each local league is chartered by the national organization and is governed by a standard set of rules and regulations. The local league is responsible for providing for its children a program with physical facilities, volunteers, and resources. Normally a local league is geared to serve a community with a fixed population of not more than 20,000 people.

A local league, if it chooses, can provide the full spectrum of baseball and softball competition for the children of its community, with players starting at age 6 and ending at age 18. In such a complete league organization, boys and girls would normally play together at the Tee Ball and Minor League level; and starting at the Little League level, the boys would play baseball and the girls would play softball. However, one of the best shortstops I saw in Little League baseball was a girl playing on her league's All Star team!

WHAT IS YOUR CHILD'S LEAGUE AGE?

League age is a term used throughout Little League that refers to the age bracket a player should be assigned to based on his or her birthday. August 1 is the official cutoff date for determining League age; for example, if your child is 12 years of age on August 1, he or she is eligible to play his or her final year in the Little League age bracket; if he or she turned 13 before August 1, the child would not be eligible for another year of Little League.

By the same token, in Tee Ball, if your child reaches the age of six before August 1, he or she is eligible to play Tee Ball for the first time; and his or her final Tee Ball year will be the year in which he or she has not reached nine years of age before August 1. Thus, ages six, seven, and eight are the three years of eligibility for Tee Ball.

LEAGUE LEVELS

League rules permit the overlapping of ages from one age bracket to another. This allows the bigger, better coordinated players to enter the next level of competition earlier than the average player. Conversely, the overlapping of ages allows the smaller, less coordinated player to have an appropriate level of competition to participate in.

The age brackets for each level of play are:

Level of Play	Age Bracket
Tee Ball*	6–8
Minor League*	8–12
Little League*	9–12
Junior League	13
Senior League*	13–15
Big League*	16–18

*Baseball and softball

A local league that provided competition at every possible level would have a total of nine divisions, each with a league vice president, managers, coaches, umpires, and many other volunteers. Sometimes field availability may be the only factor limiting the number of leagues and teams in a community. But usually a determined local board of directors will find a *Field of Dreams*–like way to accommodate all of the enthusiastic children in the community.

HOW TO START A LOCAL LITTLE LEAGUE

If there is no Little League in your community, *you* may have to be the volunteer that gets the ball rolling. Check with local schools and churches and your park/recreation department to determine cooperative interest and availability of playing fields. When you have a group of interested parents, contact your nearest regional Little League office and you will find willing and eager professionals ready to help your group. The phone numbers of the regional offices are

Eastern region	(203) 585-5137
Southern region	(813) 344-2661
Texas state	(817) 756-1816
Western region	(909) 887-6444
Central region	(317) 897-6127
Canadian region	(613) 731-3301

One thing is certain: when you advertise your first sign-up for your league, you will be surprised at the number of enthusiastic boys and girls who will show up along with their parents. Incidentally, sign-up day is the best time to enlist the many volunteers you will need in your organization, so be sure to have some members of your committee "working the crowd" to recruit parents. I recall the first time I signed up my oldest son; I was told he could play only if they found one more volunteer to manage the team he was assigned to. Guess how I got my start coaching Little League!

2
Is Youth Baseball/Softball for Your Child?

If you are a prospective Tee Ball parent, which will lead to your being a Little League Baseball or Softball parent, you are embarking on either the most satisfying or the most frustrating period of your parent-child relationship. Which it will be primarily depends on your attitude toward your child's first exposure to competitive sports. More will be said about this in the final chapter of this book, "Being an Objective Parent."

WHAT TO EXPECT

As a *minimum* commitment to your child's new sports career, you must be prepared to transport him or her to games and practices for a three-month period each spring. And you will probably be called on to help out in one or more of the parent-volunteer jobs necessary in Little League such as coach, umpire, fund-raiser, or refreshment-stand attendant.

Your child will also expect you to come to his or her

ball games and root for the team. This is where your parental objectivity is put to the test: You might see your child called out on a close play at home plate and burst into tears, but you agree with the umpire's call! Go to some Little League games and observe what is often referred to as the "Little League parent" problem. If this book accomplishes nothing else, I hope it will persuade you to remain the warm, naturally pleasant, objective person you are while watching your child's Little League Baseball or Softball game!

LET YOUR CHILD DECIDE

Is this for my child? Peer pressure may answer this question initially, and *your* pressure (for or against) ultimately. The first time you hear of Tee Ball may be when all of your child's friends are excited about signing up for their first team sport. If your child has an older brother or sister who played youth baseball or softball, he or she may provide additional motivation for or against playing.

Tee Ball is not for every child. Pity the child with "two left feet" and with a gung ho jock for a parent. Too often, Dad's attitude is "I'm going to make my kid a Little Leaguer like I was—whether he [she] likes it or not." Unfortunately "jock genes" are not always passed on from parent to child.

Conversely, you may be a parent who never participated in sports as a youngster with a child who is enthusiastic about Little League. In this case, you may discourage your child from participating because you didn't enjoy it and would be embarrassed to show your lack of coordination while helping your child. In both instances, the parent is making a decision that the child should make.

One interesting example is a father who was a jock, and whose child *had* inherited his dad's athletic ability but simply chose not to play Little League Baseball. I can recall a particular instance of this. There was a boy who moved into our community in the late fall and was an outstanding basketball player in our basketball league. All of the Little League Baseball coaches considered him their number-one prospect for the spring draft of new players but were shocked when he didn't sign up for Little League Baseball. The boy liked basketball and fishing, and Little League would have interfered with his fishing. Fortunately, his parents had the wisdom to let *him* make the choice.

My wife and I are parents of six children, three boys and three girls. In respect to the extensive variety of sports and other activities our children could choose from, we practiced the following method: expose our kids to all and encourage and assist them in any *they* wanted to try, but do not force them into what *we* might have chosen in their place. As a result, no two of the six children had the same profile of interests, and as parents we have had the mind-boggling but wonderful experience of participating in Cub Scouts, Boy Scouts, Brownies, Girl Scouts, Little League, soccer, swimming, basketball, sailing, cheerleading, music, debate, tropical fish collecting . . . and probably some others I can't recall. None of our children became a professional athlete or a musician, but they all graduated from college and have made us proud in many different ways and given us many varied, happy memories.

When I was a youth, football and tennis were my

favorite sports, and it was a great temptation to push my sons into football and all of my children into tennis. My wife was a good swimmer and a cheerleader. Nevertheless, our children did what *they* enjoyed most, including many things their parents had never done.

If neither you nor your spouse has the time to help your children in whatever they want to do because of work schedules or other legitimate reasons, explain that to them. They will understand and prefer to know *that* is the reason, rather than that you have no interest in helping them. You may be pleasantly surprised at how resourceful they can be in finding help and rides to practice once they understand that you do not disapprove.

KEEP IT SIMPLE; MAKE IT FUN!

This was the theme of my first two books on Little League, and it is no less important in Tee Ball. Perhaps it is *more* important, since "interest span" has an inverse relationship to age. Be careful not to lose patience with your child if his or her attention span for learning about the game is short. Don't falsely conclude that this means Tee Ball is not for him or her. It may only mean that through his or her behavior your child is saying, "As long as it's fun, I like it; forgive me for being young and losing interest easily." A gung ho parent can easily lose his or her patience when his or her child loses interest in playing catch after only ten minutes. The idea that "the student hasn't learned because the teacher hasn't taught" is especially true when the teacher makes practice drudgery, and not fun. Making practice a game—not a drill—is the secret, and various fun games will be explained later in this book as we discuss teaching each of the basic skills.

WHAT ABOUT THE UNCOORDINATED CHILD?

If your child is poorly coordinated at Tee Ball age, but wants to play, let him or her! Coordination comes to children at different ages. I remember a particular boy who was cruelly called "Waddles" by his peers because he was fat and walked like a duck. A more unlikely future star high school baseball player you couldn't imagine, but that's what he became. He wanted to play, his parents encouraged him, he persevered despite the taunting of his peers, and finally coordination caught up to him.

Particularly at the Tee Ball age, your youngster will have lots of company if he or she is uncoordinated. The zealous parents of an uncoordinated boy may be distressed to see girls of the same age play with much more coordination, but many girls *do* become more coordinated at an earlier age than boys. Don't let *your* embarrassment at your child's awkwardness dampen his or her enthusiasm. Children can sense a parent's disappointment, which can cause them to lose interest. Use the "sandwich" method of encouraging your child; put constructive criticism between two compliments. For example, "Boy, were we excited when you scored the first run. You need more practice catching and we'll help you, but you sure don't need any help running the bases!"

Other than a parent's negative attitude, there is little in Tee Ball to discourage the uncoordinated child. The child doesn't realize he or she is uncoordinated unless *you* say so and make him or her feel ashamed. Your youngster can happily and naively continue to have a good time in his or her uncoordinated way: surrounded by uncoordinated friends, swinging at the ball, running the bases, screaming with enthusiasm, playing what only vaguely looks like baseball—*but having fun!*

On the other hand, if your child is both uncoordinated and disinterested, it may be best to postpone his or her entry to Tee Ball. With exposure opportunities starting at age six, a year's delay is not significant. In the long run, to put if off will be more desirable than trying to force an uncoordinated, disinterested child to play. That child will be uncooperative as well. It is amazing what a difference a year can make in a child's development and coordination. I have worked with many children who

It's no fun sitting on the bench when the other kids are playing.

were overweight and uncoordinated one year, trim and well coordinated a year later.

The most important thing to consider in determining whether you should encourage your child to wait a year before entering Tee Ball is his or her attitude. What does he or she want to do? Your child may prefer to struggle through a year of Tee Ball rather than be labeled a quitter by classmates. Support your child's decision, and keep working with him or her at home. And above all, *be patient*. It may be no fun for you if you continue to see little improvement, but you are probably the only thing encouraging your child to keep trying.

If your uncoordinated child has given it his or her best shot but wants to drop out and try again next year, then let him or her, rather than forcing the child into something that is making him or her miserable. Try to expose your child to other sports or recreation he or she can do well and enjoy.

WHAT ABOUT THE BAD COACH?

Unfortunately, some would-be Little Leaguers drop out because of an experience with a bad coach at the Tee Ball or Minor League level. These levels are designed by Little League, Incorporated, to be instructional, with maximum emphasis on teaching and minimum emphasis on winning. Like all volunteer organizations, however, the willing volunteer is welcomed but seldom screened. So it is possible to have a new coach appointed who is insensitive and uncaring when working with young, impressionable children. To be fair, always make sure that your child's complaint about the coach is valid.

Observe the coach in practice, and talk to other parents who have watched him or her.

If you and other parents are convinced that the coach is bad for the children, ask the president of your league to observe him or her in practice. The president can determine whether he or she should be counseled in good coaching practices or be replaced, in an extreme case. Try to keep your concern as confidential as possible to avoid any embarrassment to your child. I have seen children cringe with embarrassment while one of their parents criticized a coach or umpire. That kind of parental behavior does not help your child have a good time. More will be said on this subject in the final chapter of this book.

A more subtle approach with an insensitive coach would be to volunteer to help him or her. Your positive influence will at least counterbalance his or her negative approach. Maybe when the bad coach sees how the players respond to your approach, you will gain a convert to a more positive coaching attitude.

PART II
TEACHING THE BASICS

3
Choosing the Right Equipment

The minimum equipment you will be expected to provide your child with for Tee Ball is a glove and athletic shoes. Additionally, if you want to go all out in helping him or her practice at home, you might get your child a baseball, a bat, a batting tee, a batting/running safety helmet, and a pitch-back net and a glove for yourself.

The equipment I am going to recommend for both practice and game use is consistent with Little League Tee Ball's standards of safety and official specifications. Although Tee Ball is not a registered trademark, in general, equipment for sale marked "Tee Ball" is appropriate. Since at-home and team practice is preparation for Tee Ball games, I recommend that the same kind of ball, bat, safety helmet, and fielder's glove that is used in games be used for practicing.

Stay away from plastic bats and whiffle balls unless you want your boy or girl to learn to play whiffle ball rather than Tee Ball. Pitch-back nets are helpful in teaching kids how to catch providing they are the sturdy kind designed for baseballs.

The baseball rests on top of the adjustable tee.

CHOOSING A BALL

"But a baseball is so *hard*," protested the mother of a six-year-old boy. "Shouldn't he first learn with a rubber ball or tennis ball?" The answer is the same as with the whiffle ball. If you want to help your boy or girl learn how to play Tee Ball, use the standard ball for Tee Ball, a slightly softer baseball marked "Tee Ball." If he or she starts learning with a baseball, no adjustment from a much softer, lighter ball is necessary.

Yes, the ball is hard, and it sometimes hurts when it hits the player instead of the player's glove. The sooner the youngster understands that, even if he or she learns it "the hard way," the better his or her concentration on catching the ball will become. "Keep your eyes on the ball" and "Look the ball into your glove" are key rules that will be emphasized throughout this book, and should be reinforced constantly during your practice sessions with your child. If he or she learns to keep eyes on the ball, the fear of getting hit by the ball will diminish. Your child won't necessarily catch all the balls, but he or she will learn to use the glove for protection as well as for catching the ball.

CHOOSING A GLOVE

Resist buying an inexpensive toy glove on the rationalization, "Maybe my youngster won't like Tee Ball, so why spend a lot for a glove?" Buying a cheap glove will guarantee that your child will not like Tee Ball because it will provide no protection at all. When the ball is caught in a toy glove with little or no padding, it will hurt!

The best glove you can get your child is a used one in good condition, one that has been broken in. If your child's older brother or sister has cast off a glove he or she has outgrown, that would be perfect—if it was not a toy glove to begin with. Or check with neighbors whose children are no longer active in baseball/softball, or look for a glove at yard sales.

You wouldn't buy shoes for your child without having them fitted. For the same reasons, don't attempt to buy a baseball glove without having your child there to try it on. Otherwise you may forget how small his or her hand is. The best place to buy a glove is a sporting goods store that stocks Little League licensed equipment. Check with your league for the name of the store where the league buys its equipment. In most cases, that store will give a discount to players from your league. But of greater importance is the fact that such a store will have knowledgeable salespeople who can properly fit your youngster with a glove.

Is it too basic to remind you that the glove is for the hand opposite the natural throwing hand? Thus, a right-handed player will want a glove fitted to his or her left hand. This in itself will seem awkward to a child who has never worn a baseball glove before. It will also seem too big, whatever size the player's hand is, and cumbersome to use, particularly if the new glove is stiff. The best type of fielder's glove from a control standpoint is the kind with a hole on the outside for the middle finger to fit through. It allows the player to gain more control in closing the glove over the ball. Go for the largest glove your child can handle; he or she will be able to use it longer, and, the larger the glove, the more balls will be caught. Have you ever looked at the size of the glove of a first baseman on a major league baseball team? He has to cover a lot of ground and uses a big glove to give himself more range.

You will hear experienced players talk about *making a pocket* in a new glove. It means treating the center

A fielder's glove with a hole for the finger is easier to control.

of the glove with linseed oil or one of the other liquids designed for this purpose. Then the ball is repeatedly thrown into the glove to gradually mold a deep pocket the size of a baseball. As long as your nerves can take the repetitive sound, this exercise can be done by your child inside the house, even while he or she is watching television.

Breaking in a new glove is something you, as a parent, can help do. Some glove manufacturers will offer pre-conditioned gloves, gloves that have been treated and mechanically broken in. They are naturally more expensive. If you break in the glove yourselves, you should buy one of the various liquids used, like linseed oil, at a sporting goods store. Usually instructions for the whole breaking-in procedure will be included.

Getting water on a new glove is the worst thing you can do, and careless youngsters who leave their gloves in the yard overnight, particularly if it rains, will find the glove stiff and cracked when it finally dries out. So if you invest in a good glove for your child, impress on him or her the importance of caring for it. By demonstrating your interest in your child's equipment, you show him or her that you share a common interest. At the same time, it gives you the opportunity to teach your child about taking care of and responsibility for his or her belongings.

CHOOSING A BAT

Although the local league will provide bats for games, your child should have one for practice at home. The bat generally used for Tee Ball is made of aluminum, magnesium, or wood. If your child has a practice bat of the

A lightweight aluminum, wood, or magnesium bat is the official bat for Tee Ball. Bats, like children, come in different sizes.

proper length and weight, that's the size bat he or she should use in the game. As in the case with gloves, resist buying a toy bat made of plastic. They are not the size, shape, or weight of a bat that can be used in a game and therefore will not help prepare your youngster for Tee Ball. It would be understandable if you asked, "Why then do major league baseball players use only wooden bats?" The answer is that metal bats are considered too dangerous at that level of play because of the 90-plus-miles-per-hour speed of a pitched ball. However, metal bats are allowed in youth baseball (including high school and college baseball) in order to give the batters an edge in a level of competition dominated by the pitching.

Don't buy a bat longer than 27 inches, no matter how big your child is. *Bat speed*, the ease with which a player can swing a bat, is more important than bat length or weight. The lighter/shorter the bat, the easier it is for a small kid to swing. Obviously the color of the bat has no importance, although you might think so, looking at the variety of colors in metal bats on the market. As in the case of choosing a glove, seek the help of an experienced salesperson in a sporting goods store that stocks Tee Ball equipment.

It is important to match player and bat. Some of these players have the wrong sized bats. The tallest player has the shortest bat, and the shortest player has the tallest bat.

CHOOSING SHOES

Because children's feet grow so fast, I would not recommend investing in rubber-cleated baseball shoes for Tee Ball. They are available, but more for good looks than practicality at that level of play. A good pair of comfortable sneakers is really all that is necessary.

Any comfortable pair of sneakers is "official." Fancy isn't better.

BATTING/RUNNING HELMET

Little League rules require that players, when batting or running the bases, and base coaches wear a protective plastic helmet. This rule applies to Tee Ball even though no pitching is done, because injuries can occur from a batted or thrown ball. Although helmets will be provided for Tee Ball games, you may want to purchase one that fits properly for your child to use when practicing at home. As he or she gets used to wearing it, it will become less of a distraction in a game. I have this mental picture of a young, short, Tee Ball batter wearing an oversized batting helmet, which covered his eyes, swinging away at a ball that he can't see. Although it is a league responsibility to provide game equipment, I suggest that your youngster uses his or her own bat and helmet in a game (even though it may seem showy). Otherwise, he or she might pick up whatever bat or helmet is available when it's time to bat, and the chances are that neither is the proper size.

The helmet can improve safety in practice if your youngster is practicing batting off the tee into a fence or the side of a building. In this situation, the ball could ricochet back and hit him or her in the head. The helmet can also provide an added element of safety when doing drills on catching fly balls.

OTHER EQUIPMENT

Most Tee Ball leagues provide a baseball cap and T-shirt. Some leagues also provide baseball-type pants. If yours does not, jeans or other long pants are advisable. Shorts are OK in hot weather, since sliding is not normally taught or encouraged at the Tee Ball level. As in the case of cleated shoes, batting gloves, wristbands, and the like are more for show than practical use in Tee Ball, and your youngster may even be called a show-off if he or she wears them.

Typically, the shortage of playing fields will limit the amount of organized practice time a Tee Ball team will be allowed to have, since they are "low on the totem pole" in comparison with the Little League and Minor League teams that use the same fields. Consequently, backyard practice may comprise a large portion of your child's practice time. If you have a pitch-back net, it will provide your boy or girl with the opportunity to sharpen his or her throwing and catching skills alone (but he or she will have more fun if you or some teammates are there). You can teach some drills that do not require supervision. They are discussed in detail later in the book. A batting drill will, of course, require the use of a batting tee. As I mentioned in the Introduction, the first batting tee I used was fashioned from an abandoned plastic road cone with a length of radiator hose serving as the adjustable ball holder. More sophisticated tees can be purchased, but make sure the vertical piece that holds the ball is adjustable up and down to the height of the batter. Teaching a level swing, the key to good batting, cannot be accomplished if the ball cannot be adjusted to the right level for the batter.

Resist the temptation to buy the best of every-thing—the fanciest glove, bat, shoes, batting gloves, wristbands, etc.—for your child's entry into organized ball. Your child's enjoyment of the sport will be mea-sured more by the time you spend than the money you spend on equipment. The amount you spend on your child's equipment may also be indicative of your paren-tal perspective, a serious subject that is addressed in the final chapter of this book.

4
Throwing and Catching

Have you ever known a youngster who, by the age of 12, did not know how to play catch? Somewhere, at some age, most kids learn how to throw and catch a ball, perhaps not gracefully but well enough to be ready and willing whenever someone suggests, "Let's play catch!"

The basic skills of baseball and softball, throwing, catching, and batting, are just that—basic skills—and they are taught in the same way as any basic skill—through repetitive drills. The most important variable in determining how early and how well a child learns these skills is the *patience of the teacher*. Sometimes an older brother or sister will try to teach a six-year-old sibling how to play catch. But having forgotten how long it took them to learn, older brothers and sisters are inclined to lose patience even sooner than parents. You also have two "interest spans" to contend with when one child teaches another. If the drill becomes boring or frustrating, it's anyone's guess which child will lose interest first.

KEEP IT SIMPLE; MAKE IT FUN!

Heard that before? You will hear it again and again. Remember that you are dealing with skills that must be taught with drills, and there is nothing like a repetitious drill to make a child lose interest. That is, unless that drill becomes fun, unless it is made a game with a way of keeping score or achieving a goal. You could see your child master the skill and, right before your eyes, be transformed from a clumsy, uncoordinated neophyte into a confident thrower/catcher. The gratification will be worth all the patience and effort you have put into it. You will have the same satisfaction that every teacher feels when a student has mastered what the teacher has taught, and more so when you are the teacher and the student is your child.

MAKING A POCKET

I am assuming you followed the advice in Chapter 3, "Choosing the Right Equipment," and have provided your child with a suitable glove and baseball, the same equipment he or she will use in a Tee Ball game (and in all subsequent levels of Little League play). Breaking in the glove was also mentioned briefly.

One drill a child can do without a teacher is to make a pocket in the new glove. Put a couple of drops of linseed oil in the center of the glove and encourage the youngster to "throw to himself," pounding the ball into the glove hand repeatedly, the purpose being to gradually mold a pocket the size of a ball into the innermost part of the glove. Inspect the glove periodically and praise your child for the progress being made at forming

Throwing the ball repeatedly into the glove will help make a pocket.

the pocket. When you are playing catch together and the ball sticks in the pocket, point out the obvious advantage of continuing to make an even deeper pocket.

As mentioned earlier, you should require your child to take good care of his or her glove and not leave it outside to be ruined by the weather. If you play catch in damp weather, be sure to have your child oil the glove when the drill is over to counteract the eroding effect of water on leather.

Sleeping on your glove is an age-old routine used by baseball players to break in a new glove. When you oil the glove, fold it and then apply weight to it: put it under your mattress and sleep on it. The process will help the glove to gradually become soft and pliable. Remind your child to put his or her glove under the mattress each night. It may also save the glove from being left outside overnight.

Be sure to stencil your child's name and phone

number on the inside of the strap on the glove. Forgetful children have been known to leave their gloves at the ball field and at neighbors' houses.

"LET'S PLAY CATCH!"

"Hey, let's play catch!" When you hear this you can rest assured that you have made that drill fun for your child.

Resist the temptation to play catch with a tennis ball or plastic ball and without a glove. That can be fun, too, but it does not teach the skill of *catching a Tee Ball baseball with a glove!* This is because catching a ball without a glove is performed with both hands equally, whereas catching with a glove is done primarily with the glove hand. The other hand has the important supporting role of keeping the ball from coming out of the glove, which differs from its role when a glove is not used. Catching a softer ball with a glove is also not the same as catching a *baseball* with a glove. The lighter weight of a plastic ball will cause frustration, since the ball will tend to bounce out of the glove. And catching a lighter ball will not help in forming the pocket in the glove. Even the sound of a baseball caught in the pocket of a glove will help to build confidence.

Fear of being hit—and hurt—by a thrown or batted ball is the greatest psychological problem to overcome when teaching a youngster to catch. There is a natural tendency for a player to turn his or her head to avoid a ball coming in his or her direction. I think it's due to the illogical notion that what you can't see won't hurt you, but unfortunately just the opposite is true. Turning the head may only mean that the ball hits the player on the

The fielder should "look" the ball into the glove and keep his or her other hand ready to cover it.

side of the head instead of the forehead, and it is dangerous in either case.

As mentioned earlier, there are two cardinal rules you must teach a youngster learning to catch. Both have to do with that all-important factor in all sports, concentration:

1. Keep your eyes on the ball.
2. "Look" the ball into the glove.

A player who keeps his or her eyes on the ball that is coming at his or her head instead of turning his or her head will learn instinctively to throw up the glove hand for protection. He or she may even catch the ball in the glove!

The two rules may seem redundant, but actually

they are different. The player keeps his or her eyes on the ball while moving his or her glove into the right position to catch it. By "looking" the ball into the glove, the player can, if necessary, make a last-second adjustment to the position of the glove to accept the ball. In any event, the glove will be positioned to protect the part of the body behind it, whether or not the ball is caught. In higher levels of play there is another rule for an infielder: Knock down the ball with the glove and keep it in front of you. Even in that situation the player is using his or her glove defensively, to protect the body from being hit.

The following is the next rule you should emphasize:

3. Cover the ball in the glove.

This is when the throwing hand is important in the

The fielder should cover the ball in the glove with his or her bare hand and get ready to pull it out for the next throw.

catching of a ball. The throwing hand should follow the ball into the glove and grip it. This has two purposes: to keep the ball from falling out of the glove and to allow the player to put the ball back into play with his or her throwing hand quickly.

USING A PITCH-BACK NET

This is the modern version of throwing the ball against a wall or some steps and catching it on the rebound. I wish I could relive the happy hours I spent as a boy doing that alone or with a friend. We made a game of it: Each caught ball was an out. Distances were marked off to indicate singles, doubles, triples, and home runs; balls caught on the fly were outs. We took turns throwing and rebounding, keeping score by innings.

The best way to use the pitch-back net with a learner is to teach a rhythm of throwing and catching starting with short distances. It teaches ball control and builds confidence in catching. The beginner has a tendency to rear back and throw as hard as he or she can, and, of course, the ball goes out of control on the rebound; sometimes the thrower misses the net completely. By teaching the thrower to aim the ball at the center of the net and throw at a controlled speed, he or she will soon develop a rhythm of throwing and catching the ball that will be very good for a beginner's confidence. When a good pace has been established at a short distance, have the player move back a few steps. Make a game out of it—for example, when your child catches five in a row, he or she moves back a few steps; when he or she misses one, your child moves forward a few steps. Keep a progress chart to see how far back from the net your child

The coach plays catch from a kneeling position with
beginners so the throw will be level.

can move each day, and keep track of his or her best
record. After your child has mastered throwing straight,
tilt the net so that it creates pop flies to catch, which is
another skill and is covered in Chapter 8.

MAKE IT FUN!

Games and personal goal setting take the boredom out
of repetitive drills. When playing catch with your child,
use your imagination to invent as many games and contests as you can. Here are a few ideas:

1. Keep score of the number of catches versus
   misses.
2. Set a goal of a certain amount of catches
   without a miss.
3. Set a goal of breaking your child's own
   record for most catches without a miss.

4. Set a goal and offer a meaningful reward: "If you break your record today, we'll celebrate at the ice cream shop!"
5. Play One Step Back, One Step Forward with the pitch-back net, as explained previously.

These are games your child can also play competitively with other youngsters.

When you teach your child to catch, your difference in height will put the child at a disadvantage. Your child will have to catch the ball thrown *down* at him or her and throw the ball *up* to you. Consequently, in the beginning, particularly at short distances, you should throw from a kneeling position to better simulate the height of the throws your child will take from his or her teammates.

GLOVE POSITION

As you probably know, the glove should be held in different positions depending on the height of the throw. As your student learns the basics of catching, add glove position to his or her repertoire. Teach your youngster the guidelines. To make a catch

1. opposite the gloved side, make a backhand catch with the glove tip horizontal
2. below the belt, the glove tip is down
3. above the belt, the glove tip is up
4. to the gloved side, the glove tip should be horizontal

Catching fly balls is an entirely different skill as mentioned above and should not be attempted until the

There are four glove positions for catching a ball. Which one is used depends on where the ball is thrown: across the body, in the dirt, above the head, or to the gloved side.

learner has mastered the basics of catching balls thrown horizontally. Chapter 8 covers the skill of catching pop-ups and fly balls.

TEACHING HOW TO THROW

When I was a kid, which was before girls were usually involved in organized baseball and softball, we used to tease the uncoordinated boy by saying he threw "like a girl." For a reason that I have never determined, girls seem to have a tendency to throw flatfooted, with their feet together. The result is an awkward throw that involves only the wrist and seldom goes very far.

A natural throwing motion involves the wrist, the

A right-hander steps toward the target with the left foot.

arm, the shoulder, the back, and even the *feet*! In order to coordinate the muscles of the arm, shoulder, and back, you must step toward the target with the foot opposite your throwing arm. Thus, a right-hander will step toward the target with the left foot while turning the right shoulder and bending the back as the right arm follows through toward the target. Follow-through is a term you will hear often in sports, particularly when throwing or pitching is discussed. If good follow-through has occurred in a throw, the index finger of the throwing hand is pointing exactly where the ball was thrown. That helps show you what adjustment must be made if the throw was off target.

To show a beginner the difference in the results of throwing flatfooted versus the correct way, have him or her throw both ways. Compare the differences in distance and accuracy. When watching a baseball game live or on TV, point out to the beginner the follow-through of a pitcher, which will be exaggerated in order to add velocity to a pitched ball.

As your child becomes a more and more accurate

Index finger of throwing hand is pointing to where the ball was thrown.

Player at left is throwing flatfooted. Player at right is stepping toward the target properly.

thrower, keep extending the throwing distance. Gradually increase it to 60 feet, which is the distance between bases. Even if the throw arrives on the first or second bounce, it will still be a good drill for accuracy in throwing to first base.

You should establish the target for throwing. Have your child aim for the head and shoulders of the person catching, since that is where the catch can be made most easily. As low as the chest is acceptable, but anywhere else will make the ball difficult to catch. Play a game called "5 and 10" with this drill. Give 10 points for a throw at the head-and-shoulder level; 5 points at the chest; 0 points anywhere else. The thrower who reaches 50 points first is the winner.

Playing catch can be a fun routine that your youngster will enjoy throughout his or her career. Even in the major leagues, the first thing the players do is play catch to warm up. If you are coaching a Tee Ball team, start playing catch with the first youngster who arrives at practice and then pair them off. Make certain that, for safety's sake, they are all in a straight line, throwing either north/south or east/west, to avoid potential injuries.

Keep in mind the limitations of a child's "interest span." Many short practice sessions are much better than a few long ones. Mix the practice drills between catching, batting, and running the bases, to provide variety and maintain interest.

And as always, "Make it simple; keep it fun!"

The only other advice I can give you is to follow the "P" rules:

Practice

Patience

Practice

Patience

Practice

Patience

Etc.

5
Batting

In Tee Ball there is no pitching, and for a good reason: the average six-, seven-, or eight-year-old has not developed the eye-hand-body-leg coordination necessary to hit a pitched ball.

It is not clear who invented the batting tee. It's a shame (for whomever it was) that he or she didn't have the foresight to have it patented, because it is now standard equipment for every baseball team, up to and including major league professional baseball teams. It is amazing how much power a well-coordinated hitter can generate when hitting a stationary ball off the tee. It is not unusual to have a well-coordinated 12-year-old hit the ball over the fence off the tee, 150 feet from home plate!

Watching some fast-paced Tee Ball games, I have noticed four common mistakes related to batting. They are as follows:

1. The tee is not adjusted to the player's height, making it impossible for him or her to achieve a level swing.

2. A player uses a wrong-sized bat. For example, a small six-year-old simply picks up
   the bat of the big eight-year-old who just
   batted.
3. A player uses a wrong-sized helmet; as in
   the situation above, the younger child ends
   up using a large helmet, which rocks loosely
   on his or her head and the peak covers his or
   her eyes.
4. The batter's feet are in the wrong position in
   relation to home plate and the tee.

These mistakes, if not corrected, can contribute to bad
batting habits.

Let's deal with each of the batting mistakes.

**Helmets come in different
sizes. A smaller one would
allow this player to see
the ball.**

Follow-through is the same in the motions of throwing and batting.

1. DEVELOPING A LEVEL SWING

At every level of competitive baseball, you will hear the batting coach encourage his players to take a level swing at the ball. A downward swing will result in a ground ball, an upward swing will result in a pop-up, but a level swing will result in a line drive, which is what every hitter strives to achieve.

"Keep your head down" is another plea made by batting coaches. If you are a golfer, you will understand. Shoulders and arms tend to follow the head. If a batter raises his or her head as the bat is brought around, the result is an upward swing instead of a level swing.

We have discussed the importance of follow-through in throwing. It is no less important in batting. As a matter of fact, the eye-arm-body coordination needed is similar. A right-handed thrower steps forward with the *left foot* as he or she brings the right arm around, and when the thrower releases the ball, the index finger of the right hand will be pointing to where the ball was thrown. In the same way, the right-handed batter will be stepping toward the pitcher with the *left foot* as he or she brings the bat around, and the tip of the bat will be pointing to where the ball was hit. The other follow-through checkpoint is the position of the batter's head. The batter's eyes should still be focused on the top of the tee the instant after he or she has hit he ball. If, instead, the batter is looking out at the field, it means the batter raised his or her head.

It should be easier for a batter to take a level swing when hitting the ball off the tee than when hitting a pitched ball, because the level of the ball doesn't change. (This is assuming the tee has been adjusted to the batter's height so that a practice level swing will just clear the top of it.) Tell that to the frustrated Tee Ball hitter who swings above the ball and misses and then swings under the ball and hits the tee. Chances are, some time you will come across a frustrated batter who can't hit the ball off the tee no matter how hard he or she tries. If possible, arrange to spend just one hour of practice time broken into 15-minute intervals to teach the child to hit the ball off the tee. That is all the time it should take for any child to acquire the basic eye, head, arm, and leg

Coach adjusts batting tee to the proper height.

coordination he or she needs to achieve a level swing and consistently hit the ball off the tee.

In the first 15-minute practice session with the batter, don't even use a ball. Establish what is the proper height of the tee for a level swing for that particular child, and use white tape to mark the stem of the tee. Put the player's number on the tape so that upon coming to bat the youngster can adjust the tee to his or her mark. Then concentrate on repetitive practice of the level swing until it becomes the child's natural, standard swing. Check the stationary position of the batter's head by lying on the ground to watch the head and eyes as the batter swings. The batter's eyes must be focused on the top of the tee, both before and immediately after the swing.

Coach lies on the ground to be able to look up and check the position of batter's eyes and head during practice swings.

2. CHOOSING THE PROPER BAT SIZE

If you followed the advice in Chapter 3, "Choosing the Right Equipment," you will have purchased the shortest, lightest bat available that is appropriate for your youngster's size. And, just as every major league ball player has his own bat(s), each child should use only a bat that is the correct size and weight for him or her. But as I mentioned earlier, in a Tee Ball game, it is not uncommon to see a batter grab the nearest bat without any consideration for its length or weight in his or her anxiety about coming up to bat. Sometimes a coach contributes to the problem by indiscriminately handing a bat just used to the next batter.

I realize that Tee Ball is not to be taken too seriously, but it *is* supposed to be an instructional league, played for the purpose of teaching kids the basics. I consider bat size/weight a basic factor in teaching a youngster how to achieve a comfortable, level swing. Once a child has reached that "comfort zone" the basic skill should become a habit through repetition. This is not possible if you let a player use a bat of different size and weight every time he or she bats. The Tee Ball coach can help each player determine what is the proper size/weight bat for him or her in practice and should advise each player to use only that size/weight bat.

3. THE BATTING HELMET

The same reasoning applies to choosing the right size batting helmet, since they come in different sizes. It is distressing to see some Tee Ball managers treat batting helmets as "optional equipment." Under Little League

It's easy for batters to choose the right sized helmet if the size is painted on the back of the helmet in large letters.

rules they are required, and a manager jeopardizes both the safety of his players and the viability of his league's insurance policy if he does not enforce that safety rule.

Helmets are not comfortable and are a distraction, particularly if they are too tight or too loose. However, the more they are worn—providing the fit is consistent— the less of a distraction they become. When I was a Little League manager, I put big letters on the back of the helmets, *S, M,* or *L.* After checking each player for the proper fit, I told them they were responsible for locating a helmet of the right size before going to the on-deck circle. Then players wouldn't be in a last-minute frenzy looking for a helmet just before going up to bat and risking getting the wrong size.

4. POSITION OF THE BATTER'S FEET

When you watch a professional baseball game, you will see a variety of batting stances, which might suggest there is no such thing as a "standard" batting stance. In the major leagues, where there are "pull hitters," "switch hitters," "opposite-field hitters," "open-stance hitters," and "closed-stance hitters," individualization is understandable. However, when teaching a six-, seven-, or eight-year-old how to bat, we are well-advised to limit our instruction to the basic "hitting up the middle." To meet that objective, the best position for the feet is to have the toes both touching a line parallel to the facing edge of home plate. How far that line should be from home plate depends on the length of the batter's arms. You want the "fat" part of the bat, the thickest part, to hit the ball. Several practice swings and much adjustment of the feet will tell you how far back the parallel

Batter draws parallel line to home plate to line up toes before batting.

line should be. With repeated turns at bat, the player should be able to sense the right distance. Some batters, either for assurance or for show, will draw the parallel line in the dirt with the handle of the bat, and then toe up to it. It makes them look like pros!

In Tee Ball, how far *back* in the box a batter should stand is an interesting question since it is the speed of a pitcher's fastball that normally determines it in higher levels of competition. Most hitting instructors suggest meeting the ball with the bat just as it reaches the front (closest to the pitcher) of the plate, because that allows

Batter draws horizontal line for anchor foot.

the batter's arms to be fully extended at the point where
bat speed reaches its peak velocity.

To translate that philosophy to the game of Tee
Ball, with a stationary ball, the batter should take a few
practice swings, and adjust his or her feet forward or
backward in the batter's box in order to feel when the
arms are fully extended and the fat part of the bat is on
the ball. Whenever the batter has found that position, he
or she can make a horizontal mark in the dirt bisecting
the parallel line to show where the back foot should be
anchored. Digging a hole there to help anchor that back
foot is what the pros do, because it is important to have

that secure anchor as all of your power shifts forward into your level swing.

In my book *Little League Drills and Strategies*, I listed 31 separate checkpoints for batters through the batting sequence from the "Ready!" position to the "Aim!" position to the "Fire!" position. I will review them here not as recommended steps for Tee Ball players but just to give the reader a complete understanding of the three-step process in the art of batting. (And you thought there were a lot of things to remember about a golf swing!)

Ready!

1. Bat is still.
2. Head is still.
3. Chin is on shoulder.
4. Shoulders are level.
5. Arms are parallel to ground.
6. Bat stays away from body.
7. Fingers are loose.
8. Knees are bent slightly.
9. Toes are on parallel line.
10. Front foot pivots toward pitcher.
11. Weight starts to shift to rear, anchored foot.
12. Arms move back.

Aim!

13. Eyes are on the ball.
14. Bat starts forward.
15. Front foot starts stride.
16. Knees turn inward.
17. Head remains still.
18. Wrists bring bat to level swing.

Fire!

19. Eyes watch ball hit bat.
20. Wrists snap at impact.
21. Weight shifts to front foot.
22. Swing is level.
23. Shoulders are rounded.
24. Hips shift.
25. Rear knee bends.
26. Rear foot pivots.
27. Back toe remains on ground.
28. Wrists roll after contact.
29. Head remains still.
30. Torso turns with bat.
31. Follow-through is smooth.

Much easier for a Tee Ball batter to remember are the Parallel Checkpoints:

Parallel Checkpoints

1. Toes are on a line parallel to the plate.
2. Shoulders are parallel. (Dipping the shoulders will move the head and make a level swing impossible.)
3. Elbows are parallel.
4. Chin is parallel and touching the shoulder.
5. Arms are parallel to the ground as they are extended in a level swing.

Batting practice is more fun than any of the other drills and will keep the interest of the child longer, provided he or she is having some success at hitting the ball. Unlike Little League, where the batter might have to wait through numerous pitches before seeing one he or she wants to hit and is successful at hitting, in Tee Ball batting practice, the ball is put in play on nearly every swing, which gives the fielders and base runners practice as well as the batter.

At a team practice, I recommend that each batter have at least five hits in succession so problems can be corrected immediately. Have other players stand by the backstop to be runners for the first four hits by the batter, then the batter will run out his or her final hit. Part of the secret of "making it fun" in team practice is having as many players involved at the same time as possible. Children at young ages seem to have more fun running the bases than any other part of practice. If there are 3 batters, 4 runners, and 9 fielders, 16 of the players will be involved in the practice at the same time. They can rotate after each batter gets five hits.

Play a batting game called "Break the Record." Have a contest in batting drills to see who can hit the ball the farthest or adapt the drill for practices with your

Coach checks the Parallel Checkpoints rules to help a batter get a level swing.

youngster. Keep a record of how far he or she hits the ball in each practice and encourage him or her to try to beat the record. Use more than one ball if possible to cut down retrieval time. You may want to record distances. You can mark distances in the field with spray paint or chalk. In this game, one player is the batter, the others are retrievers. If it is a practice with just you and your child, you will be kept very busy retrieving and marking. Having your child hit into a fence or a wall will cut down on the retrieving. This means the batter gets more times at bat per practice, but it won't work if you are practicing hitting for distance.

TEACHING GOOD BATTING HABITS

As soon as you see that a child is not hitting the ball consistently or accurately, you need to analyze the problem and correct it before bad batting habits are galvanized. Batting stance checkpoints to analyze are

1. proper size bat
2. proper size helmet
3. proper distance horizontally to the tee
4. proper distance vertically to the tee
5. hands grip the bat properly; that is, together, with the right hand on top (for a right-handed batter)
6. toes on a parallel line
7. front foot strides toward the pitcher as the bat comes through
8. head stays down with eyes focused on the spot where the ball was

Ninety-nine percent of batting problems can be traced to one or more of these eight checkpoints, with the eighth causing problems most frequently.

TEACHING SWITCH-HITTING

If your child seems well coordinated, you may want to experiment with teaching him or her to be a "switch-hitter," to be able to bat right- or left-handed. It is easier to teach switch-hitting to a six-year-old than to an older child, because a six-year-old's batting has not become so habitual that hitting from the other side seems awkward. If your child comes from an athletic family and seems destined to be an athlete in school, teaching him or her to be a switch-hitter will give the youngster a competitive advantage in making his or her school's baseball or softball team. Even at the major league level, managers will often platoon players depending on whether they are facing a right- or left-handed pitcher, whereas a switch-hitter will play every day.

Sometimes a child who seems to be naturally right-handed at writing will find it easier to bat left-handed or vice versa. There is no way you could discover it unless you give the player the opportunity to learn to hit from either side. The techniques for hitting are identical in reverse. When hitting right-handed, the batter's right hand grips the bat on top and the left foot strides forward; when batting left-handed, the batter's left hand grips the bat on top and the right foot steps forward. If something looks wrong, it could be because the batter is batting "cross-handed"; that is, with the wrong hand on top.

ON-DECK PREPARATION

In a game, a player should be told the batting order, and especially who bats ahead of him or her. When a player goes up to bat, the on-deck batter should be choosing the

The "Texas two-step" exercise helps develop
a good batting swing and follow-through.

proper bat and helmet and limbering up with practice
swings and an exercise I call the "Texas two-step." The
player puts the bat behind his or her back, resting on and
secured by his or her bent arms. Standing parallel to an
imaginary home plate, the batter takes a short step back
with his or her opposite foot, with the torso turning to
the right (for a right-hander), then a stride forward with
the same foot while the torso pivots to the left. This
simulates the leg-arm-body coordination needed in batting. It is also a good at-home drill for developing a
natural, comfortable batting motion.

6
Baserunning

How to run may seem too basic to teach a child. Believe me, it is a skill, and there are elements of this skill that need to be emphasized early so that the habits that set in are good ones. For example, the child who runs on his or her heels has to be taught early to run on his or her toes. When this skill is applied to running the bases in baseball/softball, there are running tactics that differ in a different situation. For example, the way a player runs to first base to beat out a hit is different from the way he or she runs to and around the other bases.

There is also a mental attitude regarding the bases that must be dealt with. In all other games that your children may have played, *base* is synonymous with *safe*, and being off base is risking being out. Consequently a child instinctively slows down as he or she approaches a base so that he or she does not overrun it. In baseball, however, a player *should* overrun two of the four bases, first base and home plate, and not slow down as he or she approaches them. A beginner needs to be taught to

Batter runs over first base without slowing down, being sure to touch the base.

run full speed *over* first base or home plate (touching it, of course), never breaking stride and never slowing down. It is a foot race between the runner and the thrown ball, and the runner has an advantage: in case of a tie, the runner is safe!

It is a hard concept to teach youngsters, because they have a natural tendency to slow down as they approach first base or home plate. This is especially true for beginners running to first base; they time themselves so that they can land squarely on the base *and stay there!* To run over the base and leave it is contrary to the experiences that taught them a base is a safe haven you reach and stay at. To an extent, that philosophy holds true for second and third base but not for first and home.

If you still think running is too basic to teach, line up a group of Tee Ball boys and girls and have them run

Base runner runs from third base to home plate at full speed.

a 20-yard race (the normal distance between bases), and watch the many variations of flailing arms and legs, running on heels, flatfooted, or on toes, and various positions of torsos and heads as they run.

Keep It Simple; Make It Fun!

Running is a drill that children enjoy. It is fun. As a coach, I have been known to have my players run around the bases several times just to temper their hyperactivity.

In teaching one or a group of Tee Ball youngsters, I would make a game of it by having 20-yard dashes to see who is the fastest. On the first day of practice, borrow a stopwatch and time each child on his or her first 20-yard dash in an open area. Then, after a rest, have him or her run the 20-yard distance from home plate to first base, and point out the runner's tendency to slow down, which will be confirmed by the comparative times of the two 20-yard dashes. Periodically repeat the exercise in subsequent practices after you have corrected the bad running habits, and check for improvement in the times.

One old saw about overrunning first base is that you will be tagged out if you turn back toward the infield after overrunning the base. As I will point out in Chapter 9, on rules, this is not true. A runner must make an *overt* move toward second base after crossing first base to be in jeopardy. For example, a runner who thinks he or she has a double and starts toward second base, then changes his or her mind and retreats toward first base is in jeopardy and could be called out if tagged before getting back to first base. This introduces another rule question for beginners: when does a runner have to be tagged out as opposed to being out because he or she does not beat the throw to the base? This is very confusing for beginners, and it is covered in Chapter 9.

RUNNING TO FIRST BASE

This should be taught like a foot race should be taught, particularly with respect to the finish; the runner should be like a track star breaking the tape when he or she reaches first base! If you are teaching one child, add realism to the exercise by having him or her swing the bat at home plate, pretend to hit the ball, and head for first base. One of the dangers with beginners comes when they get rid of the bat. You should clear the area of other children and fragile things. You will understand why when you encounter a child who lets go of the bat at

**Running to first base from home plate is a
20-yard foot race.**

the peak of the follow-through and it flies through the air like an unguided missile! This is the reason that during practice and games the batting area must be cleared of all players and coaches except for the on-deck batter and base coaches. They should be wearing helmets and should be instructed to always have their eyes on the batter. Although the defensive infielders do not wear helmets, they too should be coached to watch for flying bats of the metal species!

The beginner needs to be taught to *drop* his or her bat to the side of the favored hand, which will be the top hand that grips the bat on the follow-through. The batter should drop it to the side so he or she won't trip over it. The batter should not throw it and should not just let go of it during the follow-through. (Don't use bats in a group race, obviously, since dodging one flying missile should be excitement enough!)

Occasionally you will encounter a player who becomes notorious for throwing the bat. That player obviously needs special coaching to break that bad habit early, and all the players should be warned of the potential danger when the bat thrower comes up to bat.

This batter correctly drops the bat—does not throw it—as he leaves the batter's box after hitting the ball.

Batter should run to first base outside the
foul line (even if it's crooked).

RUN TO FIRST BASE
OR HOME PLATE OUTSIDE THE FOUL LINE

This is a standard rule at all levels of baseball, and it
should be taught early. The purpose for the rule is
safety—to avoid collisions between the runner and the
first baseman or other fielder. The baseline outside the
foul line belongs to the runner; the baseline inside the
foul line belongs to the fielders. The same is true between
third base and home—the runner runs outside the foul
line in order to allow the infielder to field the ball or
receive the throw. An example will illustrate why the rule
makes sense: if a batter hit an easy ground ball just
inside the first base line, and ran to first base in fair

Runner on third base runs to home plate
outside the foul line.

territory, he or she would interfere with an infielder
coming over to field the ball. In addition, if the infielder
fielded the ball after the batter had run past him or her
and the runner was running on the fair side of the foul
line, the infielder could not throw the ball to the first
baseman without hitting the runner.

NO STEALING IN TEE BALL

Stealing bases is not permitted simply because there is
no pitcher. Therefore, a base runner has to be touching
the base when the next batter hits the ball. This con-
tinues to be the rule for players who advance to softball,

but stealing is permitted under special rules in Little League Baseball.

Although in Tee Ball a runner must be touching the base until the batter hits the ball, he or she is allowed (and should be coached) to push off the base at the batter's swing to get a good start to the next base. So the base runner at first base should be instructed not to stand on the base but to take a runner's starting position in the direction of the next base, with his or her left foot on the ground, touching and ready to push off first base. In this position the runner will be looking at the batter so that the runner can push off "at the crack of the bat." The left foot is also used to push off second base, in

Runner on first base gets ready to push off when the ball is hit.

order to keep the runner facing the batter. The *right* foot is used to push off third base, again, in order for the base runner to be facing the batter.

How far and fast the base runner should push off when the ball is hit is a judgment call, and depends on whether the ball is hit on the ground or is popped up. If the base runner is "forced" at the next base (that is, if there is no empty base between the runner and the next base runner), he or she must push off on any ground ball and run as fast as possible to the next base. If the ball is popped up, the runner should push off and run a short distance, wait to see if the ball is caught, and run back to the base if the ball *is* caught. If the base runner does not run back to the base he or she had been on, the fielder who catches the pop-up could throw the ball to the baseman at that base and the runner would be out. However, if there are two outs, the base runner should be instructed to "run on anything."

NO INFIELD-FLY RULE

The infield-fly rule is found at all levels of baseball other than Tee Ball. The rule is that when there are two or more runners on base and fewer than two outs, a batter that hits a pop-up is automatically out whether or not the ball is caught. This rule does not apply in Tee Ball, so base runners have to take their chances about whether the ball is going to be caught.

The purpose of having base coaches is so they can help instruct the base runners on what to do. However, at the Tee Ball level, this player-coach may not have the foggiest notion of what to tell the base runner, so he must look to the dugout for the manager's instructions.

This is an instance in which it is an advantage for a manager to have a loud voice! He should ask the other players, and coaches, to resist using their loud voices to give advice, too. This way the base runner and base coach will not be confused by too much noise or too much coaching advice—some of which may be contradictory.

Runner rounds second base and touches bag on inside corner.

RUNNING FOR EXTRA BASES

When a batter clearly gets an extra-base hit—that is when the batter believes that a ball hit to the outfield will allow him or her to reach at least second base—the instructions for running to first base change. Instead of running *over* first base, the batter should *round* the base, touching it on the side with the foot that hits the base in stride. The same is true for a base runner who can advance more than one base on the current batter's hit. Again, the base coaches should be helping to advise the batter and base runners whether to go or stop. Hand signals are recommended since there is often too much shouting going on for the base runner to be able to pick up the coach's voice. The universal signal for a base runner to keep going is for the coach to continuously turn his extended arm like a windmill. The signal for a base runner to stop is for the coach to hold up both hands with palms extended. The first base coach gives a sign for rounding or stopping at first base; the third base coach directs runners from second to third and from third to home.

A third base-running option, to slide, is added at higher levels of play, but sliding is not taught or encouraged in Tee Ball. When sliding is permitted, the first or third base coach gives the signal. Or, if at home plate, the on-deck batter becomes the coach at home plate and signals to the runner whether to slide or come across the plate standing up.

Timing Players' Speed

As mentioned earlier, young players thoroughly enjoy running the bases, and having them do it gives them a chance to get rid of some excess energy. Sometimes as preparation for a "skull session"—that is, instruction to the group while they are sitting still—I would have them run the bases three times. Then they were too tired to do anything but sit and listen to me!

I mentioned using a stopwatch to do time trials of 20-yard dashes and to time players running from home plate to first base. Speed is usually a good indicator of who the better-coordinated players are on a team. Invariably your fastest players will also be your best athletes, and this information could be helpful to a coach in determining which players to put in key fielding spots.

Use a stopwatch to time your players as they run the bases. Have a batter swing at an imaginary ball and run the bases as if he or she had hit an inside-the-park home run. Time the player from the swing of the bat to the foot hitting home plate. Each player then has a personal time and should be encouraged to better it in future time tests.

Note the following checkpoints: Is each runner

1. keeping his or her eyes on the next base rather than looking around?
2. running with his or her torso leaning toward the next base?
3. getting rid of the bat properly?
4. running on the toes rather than on the heels of his or her feet?
5. churning his or her legs straight ahead, not to the sides?
6. swinging his or her arms from front to back and close to the body, not to the sides?
7. keeping his or her head down?
8. touching the inside corner of first, second, and third bases in stride?

"HOT BOX" DRILL

One of kids' favorite base-running drills is called "Hot Box." It requires three players, two infielders and a runner, who rotate positions. It also requires two bases (anything will serve) and, of course, a ball. The goal of the runner, who should be wearing a helmet, is to run

This runner demonstrates good
baserunning form as he nears first base.

from one base to the other (through the "hot box")
without getting tagged out. The fielders throw the ball
back and forth and attempt to tag the runner out by
trapping him or her. This drill is not recommended in
early Tee Ball training. Most six-year-olds should concentrate on just learning how to catch the ball. But more
experienced players who can catch well will enjoy it.

My son Jim went to Little League summer camp over two successive summers. The youngsters were put through a fairly strenuous schedule, with practice in the morning and two six-inning games, one in the afternoon and one in the evening. Guess what their favorite free-time activity was. It was playing "Hot Box"!

Once the players have confidence and some accuracy in throwing, this three-player drill is a good one. In it, the runner should be coached to

1. force the opponents to make as many throws as possible
2. fake direction change to force a throw
3. try to get to the other base
4. avoid the tag

The infielders should be coached to

1. make as few throws as possible
2. chase the runner back to his or her previous base
3. fake throws to force the runner to change direction
4. run the runner down rather than make another throw

7
Fielding Ground Balls and Liners

In Chapter 4, "Throwing and Catching," we introduced two important safety rules that will prevent injuries from batted or thrown balls:

1. Keep your eyes on the ball.
2. "Look" the ball into your glove.

These rules bear review in this chapter on fielding ground balls because the ground is a factor in the bounce of a ball. A batted ball that looks like it is going directly into a fielder's glove suddenly hits a stone or a high spot in the ground, and the ball heads for the fielder's nose instead of his or her glove. If the fielder has kept eyes on the ball, he or she can still get that glove in front of the face to protect the nose.

There is more infield action in a Tee Ball game than in a Baseball game since every batter gets a hit and most are grounders. It's for this reason that I frequently staged Tee Ball games as practice for my Little League Baseball team. The infielders could get a lot of action.

When lining up your players in Little League defensive positions, normally you would place your better, older players in the infield, where most of the action is. However, in Tee Ball instruction is the objective. The players should rotate positions so they all get a taste of the fast action in the infield. The only position at which you might want to be selective about placing players is first base, where the most action occurs. Taller, older, better-catching players should be placed at first base. Coaches need to use good judgment to avoid placing young or less-developed players in positions where they might get hurt.

For both safety and skill considerations, you should coach the "set" position for an infielder. The directions are as follows:

1. Spread your feet wider than your shoulders.
2. Balance on the balls of your feet; don't lean back on your heels.

Infielder fields a ground ball in proper set position.

3. Stay loose so you can shift easily in either direction.
4. Bend your legs.
5. Keep your butt down.
6. Put your hands out in front of you, about knee high.
7. Put your bare hand over the glove to form an "alligator's mouth" between upper hand and lower glove.
8. *Keep your eyes on the ball!*

The "alligator's mouth" hand position is further explained later in this chapter. When the ball is hit every infielder should *move*—either

- to the ball
  Or
- to back up the player who is going to field the ball
  Or
- to a base in anticipation of a throw there

That every player must *move every time the ball is hit* should be emphasized to the beginning fielder. Beginners have the tendency to feel that there is nothing for them to do if the ball is not hit right to them. Watching the reactions of your infielders every time the ball is hit will tell a coach whether a player is "in" the game or not. The daydreaming infielder must be identified because he or she could get hurt!

There are three common mistakes made by inexperienced infielders when fielding a ground ball. They are

1. Turning the head to avoid the ball
2. Straightening up instead of staying in a crouched position

3. "Sidesaddling" the ball—that is, reaching to
   the side for the ball instead of keeping the
   body in front of the ball

These bad habits are products of the fear of getting hit
by the ball. It can be a real problem, particularly if a
player has been hit by the ball and becomes ball shy.

"DON'T LET THE BALL GET THROUGH" DRILL

A drill called "Don't Let the Ball Get Through" can help
overcome the problem of a ball-shy infielder. It is one in
which you deliberately hit the ball at the player's body.
Tell the ball-shy infielder you don't want him or her to
catch the ball, just knock it down and keep it from going
through. Have the infielder keep the glove in front of the
face (but not covering the eyes). Then start hitting
grounders directly at the player. The infielder will find
that the ball really doesn't hurt that much when it is
blocked by the body, particularly when the face is protected with the glove. Then add to the drill retrieving the
ball and throwing it to first base. The infielder will be
learning the importance of *ball control*: if the infielder
doesn't let the ball get through, the worst that can
happen is that the batter will get a single. With a quick
recovery of the ball, the batter could still be thrown out
at first.

Naturally you would start this drill by hitting easy
ground balls directly at the infielder to build his or her
confidence. Give praise every time the ball is blocked
(with special praise when it is caught). Gradually increase the speed of the batted ball but continue hitting it
directly at the infielder. The drill can be expedited by
keeping several balls with you at home plate and hitting

Coach hits easy ground balls directly to an infielder.

them in succession. Let the infielder either block or catch each ball and then put it to the side, get ready for the next one, and wait to throw them back until you've hit them all.

As the infielder gains confidence, place more emphasis on his or her catching the ball rather than just blocking it. Make a game of it by giving the fielder 2 points for each catch and 1 point for each block. In a series of 10 batted balls, 20 would be a perfect score. Chart the player's scoring over time as he or she aims for a perfect score. If more than one player is involved in the drill, keep comparative scores to provide competitive incentive and increase concentration.

"GO GET THE BALL!" DRILL

After the infielder shows confidence in fielding balls hit directly at him or her, advance to a more difficult drill called "Go Get the Ball," which involves infielders fielding slow-rollers and balls hit to the side. "Play the ball, don't let it play you" is standard infield advice, as old as baseball itself. It is another element of ball control: players should "go get the ball" rather than waiting for the ball to come to them. Explain that you have been hitting the ball directly to infielders, but more often the ball will not be hit directly to an infielder. Fielders must move to the place where the ball can be intercepted. This means moving in on a slow-roller and moving to one side or the other.

The area to be covered by each fielder is very large. Define the fielding area of each infield position, showing each player how much area he or she is expected to cover. Show it on a diagram or on the field by drawing three lines from the center of home plate, one directly through second base, one at the halfway point between the baseline from first to second base, and the third at the halfway point between the baseline from second and third base. You will have four equally sized, pie-shaped areas, one for each of your four infielders. The fifth and sixth infielders—catcher and pitcher—should field any ball they can reach before any other infielder can reach it.

Remind them of the earlier drill in which they blocked the ball with their bodies so it couldn't get through the infield and reinforce that as the objective in this drill, too. Here are the rules to emphasize when teaching an infielder to "go get the ball":

1. Move to the ball, charging it if it is a slow-roller and moving to the spot of intercept.
2. Keep the body low in order to keep the glove low enough that the ball cannot go under the glove.

Infielder moves to intercept the ball.

Infielder gets in set position to field the ball.

Infielder "looks" ball into the glove in front of his body.

Infielder takes ball out of glove and sets his opposite foot
for the throw to first.

Infielder's hand is pointing at the first baseman at the completion of the play.

3. Keep the bare hand above the glove, palm down, so the combination of the glove hand and bare hand looks like an alligator's open mouth ready to "eat" the ball. This is what I call the "alligator's mouth" hands position.
4. Keep eyes on the ball and "look" it into the glove.
5. Pick the ball out of the glove with the bare hand and get ready to throw it.
6. Throw to first with a good follow-through, pointing to the first baseman.

Infielder uses the "alligator's mouth" hand
position so the ball will be "gobbled up" by
his glove and bare hand.

The "alligator's mouth" hands position will catch
the imagination of your child, and it has several practical
advantages:

1. If the ball takes a bad hop, the bare hand
   will be in a position to keep it from hitting
   the infielder's face.
2. The bare hand can clamp down on the ball
   in the glove, preventing the ball from popping out.
3. By gripping the ball with the bare hand, the
   infielder is ready to make the throw to first
   base.

DIVE DRILL

Frequently balls hit are neither ground balls nor fly balls. These are normally referred to as "liners," and a good infielder can often catch them before they hit the ground. Catching a liner not only will result in an out, but it could result in a double play if there are runners on base.

The Dive Drill is simple but tiring. The coach tosses liners (or hits them if he or she is skilled enough) to the left or right of the positioned infielder. The player doesn't know whether the ball is coming to his or her left or right, so he or she has to be ready to dive in either direction. Since the fielder usually ends up flat on the ground after the catch—or attempted catch—start the drill in grass to cushion the fielder's fall. Gradually move it to a dirt infield for realism as the player gets the knack of it. Keep score, and again allow 5 points for a catch and 3 for a block.

Coach makes infielders dive for the ball.

MAKING THE THROW TO FIRST BASE

The infielder has made half an out when he or she successfully fields the ball. The other half of the out involves making an accurate throw to first base. Since Tee Ball games are played on the same sized fields as Little League games, with 60 feet between the bases, it is understandable if a six-year-old Tee Ball shortstop can't make the throw to first base as easily or as accurately as his 12-year-old counterpart in Little League. Even in the major leagues these days, better shortstops are using the one-bounce throw to first base when their throw has to be a long one. So if the Tee Ball shortstop gets the ball to first base on a two-bounce throw, that isn't too bad. Accuracy should be stressed rather than the velocity of the throw. This is another example of the importance of ball control, since frequently accuracy is sacrificed when velocity is great.

The mechanics of making a throw from an infield position to first base are the same as they are in a game of catch, but first the fielder must get control of the ball by

1. "looking" the ball into the glove in a crouched position
2. clamping the bare hand over the ball so it doesn't pop out
3. getting a grip on the ball with the throwing hand as he or she comes out of a crouch and focuses on the target at first base

Many embarrassed infielders have started to make the throw before they have control of the ball. This results in no throw because the ball has gotten past the infielder. It usually happens when the infielder straightens up too soon and does not "look" the ball into the glove. The glove comes up off the ground as the body straightens up, and the ball goes between the infielder's legs under the glove. A ball-shy infielder is particularly guilty of rising out of a crouched position too soon because he or she is afraid of getting hit in the face with the ball. The ball-shy infielder needs special drilling on using the "alligator's mouth" hands position to overcome this fear.

Keep emphasizing the importance of ball control to your child. Tell the child that it isn't necessary to field the ground ball cleanly every time, but it is necessary to control the ball by blocking it with your body and keep it in front of you. Remind your child that sometimes a good throw to first base can be accomplished just as well after picking up a blocked ball as it can after pulling the ball out of the glove.

THROWING TO THE OTHER BASES

A beginner learns quickly that the batter running to first base is out if a defensive player's throw to the first baseman, whose foot is touching the base, gets there before the batter does. But it gets a little complicated when you try to explain to a beginner that putting a runner out at the other bases can be different. For example, sometimes the infielder has to tag the runner with the ball instead of just touching the base. There are even cases in which the infielder should tag the runner *before* he or she reaches first base rather than risk a throw to first base (such as if the pitcher fields the ball near the first base foul line as the batter-runner is approaching).

To tag or not to tag the runner is a player's decision dictated by the rules. Even major league players will blow it occasionally. I have a painful memory of a 12-year-old catcher on our Little League team who was clearly the best catcher in the league, yet who blew a play in a championship game. In a tied game, there were opposing runners on second and third bases with one out. The batter hit a bounce-back to the pitcher, who, seeing the runner on third breaking for home plate, threw the ball to our catcher. The throw beat the runner by ten feet, but instead of tagging him, the catcher just stepped on home plate thinking the bases had been loaded.

For six-, seven-, and eight-year-olds—beginners with short memory spans—the best rule for tagging or not tagging the runner is "When in doubt, tag the runner." Emphasize to the players that if you are a baseman with your foot on the base, and the ball is thrown to you before the runner reaches your base, *tag the runner*. If the runner was forced, you don't get two outs, of course, but you will have made sure that you got one out.

8
Catching Fly Balls

I would not recommend teaching how to catch fly balls until your youngster has fairly mastered catching horizontal throws in games of catch. You can work into it by putting a slight arc on your throws, but keep in mind that as you do you increase the danger of the child getting hit on the head. Judging a ball coming down from a height is a different skill altogether.

In the beginning you may want to take two precautions when teaching a kid to catch fly balls:

1. Have the player wear a batting helmet as protection.
2. Use a tennis ball or rubber ball at first.

I realize that prescribing the use of a softer ball may appear to contradict what I said earlier, but this is the only teaching sequence for which I would make that recommendation, and I do only temporarily. The reason to use a softer ball at first is simple: The beginner will initially misjudge fly balls and *will* get hit on the head, shoulder, or arm. And getting hit by a tennis or rubber ball won't hurt as much as getting hit with a baseball.

The glove should be worn even with the softer ball, and the bare hand should be used to cover the ball so it doesn't pop out of the glove. A lighter ball will have a tendency to pop out more, so one consolation is that when you switch to a Tee Ball baseball it should improve the player's percentage of catches. I recommend switching to a baseball as soon as you think your child has developed some confidence.

POP-UPS

Pop-ups are fly balls hit straight up into the air, usually in the infield area, as opposed to long, arcing fly balls hit to the outfield. Pop-ups give the fielder the advantage of having more time to locate and get under the ball, but they do have their own peculiar problems. A ball coming straight down at a player can force the player to look into the sun or can be affected by wind currents.

"I'VE GOT IT, I'VE GOT IT!"

There is always a question of who should catch a fly ball or pop-up and the danger of players colliding with each other, especially in the infield where the players are grouped fairly close together. As soon as a player feels he or she has the ball under control the player should call out loud and clear, "I've got it, I've got it," and the other player(s) should get out of the way. One can serve as a backup. There is a basic rule for determining who should catch the ball when choices are between an infielder backing up and an outfielder coming forward. Assuming they both have a shot at it, the player coming forward should call for it, because he or she has a better chance of catching it.

In addition to calling for the ball, the player should wave his bare hand back and forth so the other players will see as well as hear that he or she intends to catch the ball. This is not a situation that requires politeness. If two players are vying for the ball, both players should continue to attempt to catch the ball until one or the other calls for it. Sometimes neither one can get to it, which makes it all the more important that they both continue to run to where it falls, so the nearest one can retrieve the ball and throw it in.

I tell players to use the "camera method" to judge a fly ball or pop-up. If you were going to take a picture of the ball (or catch it) you would have to focus on it. And

This infielder uses the "camera method" to judge a pop-up. His eyes are focused on the ball.

Fielder has both hands ready to catch a fly ball.

since it is moving, you have to *keep it in focus* while you reach the best position to catch it. This is called *concentration*; it is *keeping your eyes on the ball!*

I recommend telling the beginner to use the index finger of his or her bare throwing hand to point to the ball so his or her eyes can follow the focus. That will get both hands in the air, which is the proper position for the hands when preparing to catch a fly ball. The hands should also be close to each other so that when the ball falls in the glove, the bare hand can cover it and prevent it from popping out and then grip the ball for the throw.

A DRILL FOR CATCHING POP-UPS

A drill for catching pop-ups should start with the coach throwing the ball a short distance into the air so that it comes down directly to the player. Then gradually increase the height. Then start varying the location where the ball lands so that the player has to move under the ball to catch it. The same kinds of games and contests that were suggested in Chapter 4 for playing catch can be organized to "keep it fun." For example, make a note of the greatest number of catches without a miss and try to break the record, make each player catch five in a row at one difficulty level before moving to the next level of difficulty, and so on.

There is probably no skill easier to teach with repetitive practice than the skill of catching a fly ball or popup. Yet you often see children even at the Little League level avoid catching a fly ball—even running in the opposite direction to be sure they are not anywhere near it when it falls to earth! It is a sure sign that the coach of that youngster has not had the patience to teach him or her how to catch a fly ball.

A coach will have a real sense of accomplishment

Coach hits tennis balls to beginners with a racket to teach them how to position themselves to catch fly balls.

when he or she has shared the skill of catching a fly ball with an uncoordinated youngster. Only lack of patience and perseverance will prevent you from doing it. Once learned, the youngster will keep that skill for life. With children I have coached, I would usually get physically tired from hitting fly balls in practice before they would tire of catching them.

The pop-up drill progresses from throwing tennis balls in the air to hitting them with a tennis racket, which increases the level of difficulty since the fielder will not know where the ball will be hit. A coach's use of a tennis racket also makes it easier for him or her to control the ball. When your student has developed confidence in catching the tennis ball hit with the racket, begin using a baseball for the drill. Work through each level of difficulty again. Gradually increase the difficulty of the throws and the balls hit with a racket the same way you did with the tennis ball.

CATCHING FLY BALLS

In some ways, catching a fly ball hit on a predictable arc is easier than catching a pop-up, although at first catching a fly ball will seem like an impossible task to a beginner because the ball is hit so hard and so far. Focusing on or sighting the ball is the first priority. The ability to catch a fly ball will come only with experience and after misjudging many fly balls. A fielder will learn from the ones misjudged so that gradually his or her judgment will become better and better through practice.

For a drill on catching fly balls, have outfielders wear batting helmets. Throw a tennis ball instead of hitting it at first so you can better control it. When your

The accuracy of the throw back in after catching a fly ball is as important as the catch.

players' confidence in catching the tennis ball has been developed, switch to a baseball, starting again with throws from short distances and gradually increasing difficulty.

KEEP IT SIMPLE, MAKE IT FUN!

After he or she catches a fly ball, a player has to throw it back in, and the accuracy of the throw is as important as the accuracy of the catch. In a game situation, the outfielder throws to the relay person (usually the shortstop or second baseman), and that player throws to the base where the play is to be made. As a rule of thumb, I have always coached my players to throw two bases ahead of the runner on a hit and one base ahead of the runner on a caught fly ball. For example, if there is a runner on first and the batter gets a single, the outfielder should throw to third base; if the batter hits a caught fly ball, the outfielder should throw to second base. This may be too advanced for Tee Ball players, who will have to rely on their coaches to tell them where to throw the ball.

We make a game out of learning to catch fly balls and throw and catch accurately in practice by organizing three-player teams, each with one adult coach. The three players alternate playing the outfield, relay, and catcher positions. We work through a hypothetical game situation. We say there is a runner on third who will attempt to score after a fly ball is caught. The outfielder has to

Coach hits fly balls in a three-player drill
with outfielder, cutoff person, and catcher.

catch the fly and quickly get the ball to the relay person, who then fires it to the catcher at home plate. Use a scoring system of 3 points for a catch, 1 point for an accurate throw to the relay person, and 1 point for an accurate throw to the catcher. In addition to playing a competitive game among the teams of three players, you are developing three skills. Best of all, they think it is fun!

9
The Fundamental Rules of the Game

Tee Ball is *sort of* like baseball . . . but the only thing about it that is *identical* to baseball is the size of home plate! Bob Newhart could have made a hilarious skit about trying to explain to someone about a baseball game for children in which there is no pitching, you don't keep score, there is no base stealing, every batter bats in every inning, and children six, seven, and eight years old play it!

Many people would doubt that there could be such a game—after all, everyone knows that pitching is at least 50 percent of the game of baseball. But those doubters would become believers when they found out the number of parents who watch and if they heard the whooping and hollering that goes on among the children who play. And that's why it has become such a popular sport: the kids have fun playing it!

Tee Ball is seriously related to baseball in that it teaches the basic skills of throwing, catching, batting, and running the bases and that it is loosely organized into some rules that are also, well, sort of like baseball. There is no pitching because children six to eight years old are not coordinated sufficiently to pitch a ball consistently in the strike zone or to hit a ball that *anyone* pitches in the strike zone. There is no base stealing because there is no pitching. Keeping score is not important because Tee Ball is an instructional league dedicated to giving every child the opportunity to learn and play. Can you name any other organized sport where that is true? In Tee Ball, nobody cares who wins as long as everybody has a good time. And believe me, they do!

All of that might indicate that nobody really cares about rules in Tee Ball. But let me assure you that there is a defined purpose and some rules and regulations for Tee Ball, which are established by Little League, Incorporated. The rules listed are the exceptions to those of higher levels of Little League. They are specific to Tee Ball and are designed for the safety of the children and to guarantee that the defined purpose is achieved.

Little League® Tee Ball

Regulations

The following regulations must be applied to a Tee Ball program operating under a Little League charter.

1. The Tee Ball program must operate under the direct supervision and control of the parent Little League Board of Directors.
2. Boundaries from which participants are selected must be identical to those currently chartered by the parent Little League program.
3. Tee Ball rosters shall not exceed 20 players; however, it is recommended that Tee Ball rosters not exceed 15 players. At least one or more qualified adults should supervise a Tee Ball team.
4. Assignment of Tee Ball players should be a cooperative effort of managers, coaches and the player agent following an appropriate player evaluation try-out session. It is recommended that teams have an equal number of players of each age.
5. Managers shall draw for teams after player assignments have been completed.
6. Tee Ball rosters may be readjusted at any time during the season at the direction of league personnel.

Players

1. Tee Ball may be offered for players 6, 7 and 8 years old, and must utilize the "batting tee" rather than the pitched ball.
2. Any candidate who will attain the age of 6 years before August 1 and who will not attain the age of 9 years before August 1 of the year in question shall be eligible to participate in the Tee Ball program.
3. The league president must certify and be responsible for the eligibility of each candidate prior to player assignments.
4. "League Age" is that age attained prior to August 1 in any given season. Thus a youngster whose 8th birthday is on July 31 or earlier has a League Age of 8; a youngster whose 8th birthday is on August 1 or later has a League Age of 7.
5. The "League Age" of each participant shall be recorded and announced during player assignment to guide league personnel.

Schedules

1. The schedule of games for Tee Ball shall be prepared by the Board of Directors. An appropriate number of games shall be scheduled in conjunction with field availability.
2. It is recommended the schedule provide for not more than two games per week.
3. If a Tee Ball program plays a schedule of games or operates as an instructional program, it must dissolve at the conclusion of the current season. All players are returned to the league's player pool.
4. It is recommended no league standings be kept or championship games be played.

Special Games

Special Games are permissible in Tee Ball only with regular season teams; however, they are not recommended by Little League Headquarters.

Night Games

1. The playing of night games under artificial lights is contrary to Little League principles, but may be played for justifiable reasons.
2. The responsibility of playing Tee Ball under artificial lights rests with the local league. In any event, no inning shall start after 9:00 P.M. prevailing time. It should be noted that an inning starts the moment the third out is made, completing the preceding inning.
3. Artificial lights for Tee Ball must meet minimum standards approved by Little League. (See President's Handbook.)

Equipment

1. All protective equipment, bats and balls used in the Tee Ball program must meet Little League specifications.
2. All batters, base runners, base coaches and "on-deck" batters must wear protective helmets.
3. The player occupying the defensive position of catcher must wear full protective equipment including a catcher's mask and protective helmet, shin guards and long model chest protector with neck collar. All male catchers must wear the plastic, metal or fiber protective cup.
4. It is recommended that Tee Ball programs use only T-shirts and caps as uniforms.

Admission

No admission shall be charged to any Tee Ball game. Voluntary contributions are permitted.

Awards

No awards shall be made to players on the basis of comparable skills or accomplishments in Tee Ball. Player participation certificates may be presented at the conclusion of the season.

Commercialization

1. A reasonable Tee Ball participation fee may be assessed as a parent's obligation to assure the operational continuity of the Tee Ball program. Although it is recommended that no fee be collected, a maximum of $20.00 per player may be assessed if deemed necessary. **At no time should payment of any fee be a prerequisite for participation in a Tee Ball program**.
2. Separate fund raising by Tee Ball programs is prohibited.

Field Decorum

1. The actions of players, managers, coaches, umpires and league officials must be above reproach.
2. Players, managers, coaches and umpires should only occupy the confines of the playing field and dugouts prior to and during the games.
3. Except for the batter, base-runners, the player "on-deck" and coaches at first and third bases, all players shall be on their benches in their dugouts when the team is at bat. When the team is on defense, all reserve players shall be on their benches in the dugout.
4. Managers and coaches may stand near batters and defensive players to offer advice, but shall not interfere with play. The manager or coach shall request "time" from the umpire before demonstrating a technique or explaining a situation to the players during the progress of a game.
5. Batboys and/or batgirls are not permitted.
6. The use of tobacco and alcoholic beverages in any form is prohibited on the playing field, benches and dugouts.

Television

The televising of Tee Ball games is prohibited.

Tournament Play

Tournament games involving All-Star teams in Tee Ball are prohibited.

Recommended Playing Rules

Objectives

1. Tee Ball is a game between two teams of nine or more players, where participants hit a ball off a prescribed batting tee situated on home plate.
2. The Tee Ball playing field should be identical in dimensions to a Little League field; however, it is recommended base paths be 50 feet in length.

Game Preliminaries

1. Managers and coaches may be used as umpires.
2. The local league will establish ground rules to be followed by all teams in the Tee Ball program.

Putting the Ball in Play

1. When all defensive players are in proper position the defensive manager will indicate to the umpire his team is ready. The umpire will then place the ball on the tee and say, "Play ball."
2. It is recommended that the defensive team consist of nine players (baseball) or ten players (softball).

Definition and Application of Terms

Batting Order—The batting order shall be the players listed in the order they are to bat. The batting order shall contain the entire roster of players. Batting orders need not be exchanged between managers prior to the start of the game.

Mandatory Play—All players listed on the roster shall play defensively for at least one inning and bat at least once.

Base Runner—Base runners must stay in contact with the base until the ball is hit. When players have advanced as far as possible without being put out, or having been retired, the umpire shall call "time" and place the ball on the tee.

Side Retired—The offensive side is retired when three outs are made or when all players on the offensive team have batted one time.

Foul Ball—Identical to conventional baseball with two exceptions: (1) The ball is foul if the ball travels less than 15 feet in fair territory from home plate, and (2) the ball is foul if the batter hits the tee with the bat causing the ball to fall from the tee.

Strike Out—The local league will determine whether or not strike outs will be permitted in Tee Ball.

Hitting—The batter should not be permitted to bunt or take a half-swing. If, in the umpire's judgment, the batter does not take a full swing, he may call the batter back to swing again.

Defensive Substitution—The manager of the defensive team is permitted to use free substitution at any time during the game when the ball is not in play.

Infield Fly—The Infield Fly rule does not apply in Tee Ball.

Protest—There shall be no protests in Tee Ball.

Forfeit—There shall be no forfeits in Tee Ball.

Regulation Game—The local league may determine appropriate game length, but should not exceed 6 innings. It is recommended Tee Ball games be 4 innings or a one and one-half hour time limit imposed.

Apply the Rules as Guidelines

Although some of the foregoing rules seem rather prescriptive, local leagues do have some flexibility as long as the purpose of Tee Ball as an instructional league is not compromised. Some of my comments in this book have been influenced by the way our local Tee Ball organization operates. For example, we have used the option of having each half inning consist of every player on the team batting rather than have it consist of three outs, because we felt strongly about giving every child the opportunity to play. We have also been known to have more than nine players in the field for the same reason.

When your child advances to Little League, play will be governed by the *Little League Baseball Official Regulations and Playing Rules*, a 64-page document in fine print. Most of the rules are common to baseball at all levels, and accordingly they are very precise. In regard to those regulations and rules and the foregoing Tee Ball supplement, which outlines special provisions for the Tee Ball level of play, I have narrowed down what I think Tee Ball players need to understand to 11 subjects.

Mandatory Play

A player shall play defensively for at least one inning and bat at least once. However, there is little justification, in my opinion, for a Tee Ball manager not to go beyond the minimum requirement and give every player *equal* playing time.

Use of Protective Equipment

Seven batting helmets should be provided. This is to accommodate the maximum number of people required to wear them at any one time. They are the batter, three base runners, the on-deck batter, and two player-base coaches. If your Tee Ball league is not complying with this very basic safety rule, you should complain. Also, even though there is no pitching, a catcher is still vulner-

A Tee Ball catcher should be provided with
the same full protection equipment as a
Little League catcher even though there is
no pitching in Tee Ball.

able to being hit by foul balls and thrown bats and
falling over the tee. Catchers should be provided with
full protective catcher equipment.

Foul Balls

A foul ball is a batted ball that settles on foul territory
between home and first base or between home and third
base, that bounds past first or third base on or over foul
territory, or that while on or over foul territory touches
the person of an umpire or player. In Tee Ball there are

two additional definitions of a foul ball. A foul ball in Tee Ball is

1. a ball that is hit and travels less than 15 feet in fair territory from home plate
2. a ball that falls from the tee because the batter hits the tee

It should be pointed out to infielders that, as a basic part of defensive strategy, they can sometimes control whether a ball hit along the first or third baseline is fair or foul. If the ball is hit into fair territory but is heading for foul territory, it will be ruled fair if the fielder touches it in fair territory even though it subsequently rolls into foul territory. In such an instance, if the fielder is certain he or she can make an out, the ball should be retrieved. Conversely, if the fielder feels certain he or she can't make an out, the ball should be allowed to roll across the line into foul territory.

Batter and Runner Out When Hit by a Batted Ball

A batter is out if he or she comes in contact with a fair ball before it touches a fielder. A runner is out if he or she is touched by a batted fair ball before the ball is touched by or passes an infielder. Your youngsters should be warned to avoid touching a batted ball when they are running the bases.

Runner Interference

A runner is out if he or she intentionally interferes with a thrown ball or hinders a fielder from attempting to make a play on a batted ball. Your youngsters should be warned to avoid touching a thrown ball or keeping a fielder from catching the ball.

Fielder Obstruction

A fielder may not prevent a runner from running unimpeded to the next base.

Two Runners May Not Occupy the Same Base

When it happens—and it will—a fielder should tag the second runner and he or she will be out.

Two runners may not occupy the same base. The second runner is tagged out.

Tagging Up on a Caught Fair or Foul Ball

A runner may advance to the next base at the risk of being tagged out before he or she gets there if he or she leaves the previous base *after* a fly ball (fair or foul) is caught.

Force Play

Whenever a base runner is forced to advance because the batter has put the ball in play and become a runner, the first runner is out if he or she fails to reach the next base before being tagged or the base is tagged. My advice, as mentioned in Chapter 6, is to coach your players to tag the runner *and* the base when in doubt as to whether or not it is a force play.

Overrunning First Base

A batter-runner cannot be tagged out after overrunning first base if he or she returns immediately to the base.

Runner Leaving Base Too Soon

There is no stealing in Tee Ball. The runner must stay in contact with the base until the ball is hit.

PART III
KEEPING A GOOD PERSPECTIVE

10
Making Practices Fun

Helping your child learn to play a game he or she wants to learn can be one of the most gratifying and memorable parent-child experiences of your life and your child's life. It is quality time spent together, and the memories will be cherished by you both.

However, there is a "generation gap" that must be recognized and dealt with. We parents sometimes have vague or distorted memories of our own childhood, or we try to relive a pleasant memory of our childhood with a child that doesn't have the same interests or level of intensity. What your child wants to do in sports is more important than what you want him or her to do.

The acid test of the generation gap occurs between your patience and your child's "interest span." The secret to making it work is to "keep it simple; make it fun." If your youngster tires quickly of the practice sessions with you, it may be because the teacher isn't teaching— not that the student isn't learning—or that the teacher isn't allowing for the short "interest span" of a six- to eight-year-old.

Variety is also "the spice" of practice, and the key to the objective "keep it simple; make it fun" is to vary the drills and switch when you sense a child's interest in the one you are doing is waning. The following is a suggested outline for a parent-child practice session. I have deliberately avoided recommending a time span for each because you will have to be the judge of your child's interest, which varies greatly among children in the six- to eight-year-old age range.

CATCHING PRACTICE

Playing catch will probably be the first "game" you suggest, since it provides some "limbering up" value for both parent and child in addition to practice of both throwing and catching. These two basic skills are thor-

Coach plays catch with a beginner from a kneeling position so throws will be level.

Fielder "looks" ball into the glove.

oughly discussed in Chapter 4 and briefly reviewed here.

Before you start, inspect your child's glove to make sure it is fitting snugly and has a pocket. Kneel on one knee so that your throws will be level and not downward to your child. Watch his or her head to make sure your child is not turning it as the ball approaches, and don't increase the distance between you until your child is comfortable with the previous distance. Keep stressing the three important rules of concentration in catching:

1. Keep your eyes on the ball.
2. Look the ball into your glove.
3. Cover the ball with your bare hand.

If your child gets into the bad habit of making one-handed catches, after watching the professional ball players do it on TV, offer this advice: "Those pros started catching with two hands, and when you get as good as they are, you can start catching one-handed, too."

Every time your child catches the ball, *be generous*

with your praise! Your recognition and encouragement will help make it fun and encourage your child to strive for the next level of achievement.

Introducing games within the game of catch will also enhance your child's enjoyment. Some of these games, such as One Step Back, One Step Forward and keeping track of the number of catches versus misses are described in Chapter 4, but the number and variety of them are limited only by your imagination.

Be sure to check the throwing, as well as the catching, technique and be patient if your child has trouble throwing the ball right back to you. Be sure he or she is stepping toward you with the opposite foot from the throwing hand and is pointing at you after the follow-through. Introduce the game of "5 and 10" (see Chapter 4) as your child improves in throwing accuracy.

On the nights you or a friend of your child's can't practice with him or her, using a pitch-back net will enhance his or her ball control. As explained in Chapter 4, you will need to teach your child how to use the net. Just as in playing catch with you, he or she should start close to the net and throw at a speed that will allow him or her to react properly when catching the ball. And also just as in playing catch, keeping track of the number of catches versus misses in each series of 10 throws from each distance will make using the pitch-back net more fun.

BATTING PRACTICE

This is the practice your youngster will enjoy the most— after he or she learns how to bat properly. The sheer delight of swinging the bat, hitting the ball squarely, and seeing it fly off the tee on a line drive—that will keep bringing your child back for more! In contrast to throwing, with which we caution the beginner not to rear back and throw with all his or her might until control and accuracy are mastered, batting is a skill that the youngster can attack with a vengeance—once you have worked with him or her on a few basics of technique. These basics are explained in Chapter 5 and reviewed briefly here:

1. Determine the proper height of the tee and use numbered tape to mark the stem of the tee clearly so that height can be set every time the child bats.

2. Pick the lightest bat the child can comfortably swing.

3. Make sure the batting helmet is the correct size and does not move during the swing, which would cause a distraction and possibly interfere with sighting on the ball.

4. Check position of batter's feet. They should be parallel to the edge of home plate and at the proper distance from the tee to allow the fat part of the bat to hit the ball.

5. When the batter takes practice swings without a ball, check to make sure that the head is kept down and the eyes are focused on the top of the tee even after the bat has swung past.

6. Check to be sure that the batter strides toward the pitcher's mound as he swings and does not bat flat-footed.

7. Check to be sure that the batter's rear foot is anchored.

Remember, keep it simple; make it fun! Keeping it simple will be the more difficult assignment, because those seven batting checkpoints must be constantly checked and rechecked. When even major league batters go into a hitting slump, it is usually because they got careless or lazy about one or more of the basic mechanics of batting.

There are two backyard batting practice drills you can organize for your child, and he or she will love them. Both require a batting tee, a batting helmet, a bat, and balls (as many as you can afford, to save time and effort in retrieving batted balls).

Hit the Target! Drill

In this drill the batter hits into a backstop, a fence, or a wall starting from a distance of about ten feet and gradually increasing the distance. Construct a target by painting concentric circles on a square piece of cloth. Paint a bull's-eye in the center, where a level swing would produce a line drive, straight up the middle. You can assign points for hitting the bull's-eye and for hitting surrounding circles and keep score on a set of 10 hits.

The purpose of this drill is to emphasize batting skill and consistency, not distance (which is the next drill). When a youngster demonstrates mastery of batting basics such as swinging level, keeping the head down, and the others as listed, he or she should be able to consistently hit the bull's-eye. The most difficult variables at higher levels of baseball, ball speed and position, are not factors in Tee Ball hitting, which allows for more concentration on the non-variable basics. In Tee Ball, the ball is always in the same position and at no speed,

Coach works with batter on the backstop
hitting drill.

which makes the basic mechanics habit-forming, if the
player has plenty of practice and if there is plenty of
patience exercised on the part of both teacher and student.

Hit for Distance! Drill

This drill requires a setup in which the batter hits into a
baseball diamond or open field with a standard swing off
the tee from home plate. Markers can be placed in the
field to indicate distances from home plate, or the farthest hit can be marked and the mark only changed when
a longer hit occurs. The spot should be marked where
the ball hits the ground, not where it stops rolling. A

Batter gets ready to hit for distance.

variation on this drill is to line off the field for singles, doubles, triples, and home runs.

Switch-Hitting Drill

As mentioned in Chapter 5, letting a child practice hitting from both the right and left sides at an early age will give the player the opportunity to try switch-hitting before it becomes awkward or, better said, while the youngster can do it with a degree of awkwardness equal from the right or left side. Have each player hit 10 balls from the right side and then 10 from the left and see which side will produce the best hits.

BASE-RUNNING PRACTICE

You should use a stopwatch or the second hand on your watch to time your child as he or she runs two races "against the clock." You might want to keep a record of the times to track your child's improvement on the following three drills.

Running to First Base Drill

This drill is a 20-yard dash from home plate to first base. If you're not practicing at the field, make it as realistic as possible by marking off the distance using markers for home plate and first base. Make the batter wear a helmet, swing at an imaginary ball on the tee, pretend the ball was hit to the infield, and proceed as if he or she has to race to first base to beat the throw! This exercise will give you the opportunity to check the child's performance on a number of batting and base-running basics such as

1. level bat swing
2. head down and eyes on the ball
3. proper release of the bat
4. eyes on first base
5. arms swinging forward and backward
6. legs churning straight ahead
7. running on toes, not heels
8. running on foul side of foul line
9. running over first base without slowing down
10. touching first base

When taking pictures of Tee Ball players running to first base for this book, we were amused by how many varied running styles there were and by how many players did everything right except touching first base.

Running the bases is a simple drill that players enjoy, and it helps work off excess energy.

Running the Bases Drill

After teaching your youngster to run to first base as if it was a 20-yard dash, teach him or her to circle the bases, making a wide turn at first base and just touching it on the near corner. "Which do I do?" would be a logical question, and the answer is "It depends." Coach your child to do the following:

- On any ball hit to the infield (on the ground or in the air), race to first.
- On any ball hit to the outfield, make the turn at first base, being sure to touch the corner of the base. Then look at where the ball is and listen to your coach, who should be telling you whether or not to continue to second base.

Inside-the-Park Home Run Drill

Speed is an important part of running the bases, so another drill is to have batters swing at imaginary balls and then run around the bases as though they've hit inside-the-park home runs. Keep a record of the time it takes each player to round the bases at each practice, and encourage them to try to better their own best times. Check to make sure every base is tagged on the inside corner by each runner. Beginners will have trouble adjusting their strides so they can hit the inside corners of the bases with their right feet. Doing it right requires practice, practice, practice, but their speed will improve when they master it.

Sometimes a beginner forgets which way to run the bases.

FIELDING GROUND BALLS AND LINERS PRACTICE

Three infield drills—the "Don't Let the Ball Go Through" Drill and the "Go Get the Ball" Drill for grounders and the Dive Drill for liners—are described in Chapter 7. These drills can be done separately or integrated into one infield drill. Monitor your child for the eight checkpoints in Chapter 7 that ensure that he or she is making a habit of the mechanics of fielding grounders. The most important—and the most violated—of these checkpoints is to "keep your eyes on the ball" as you "look" it into your glove. It is also very important to keep down: body down, butt down, hands down, head down. Because carelessness in these important mechanics is caused by fear of getting hit by the ball, blocking the ball should be integrated with drills for fielding the ball. The more children use their body to block the ball, the less fearful they will become. They will discover that it really doesn't hurt *that* much, and so long as they keep their eyes on the ball, they can use their glove, their body, or both to keep the ball from hitting their face.

After you have hit enough grounders directly at your child and his or her catching/blocking is getting good, then make the task more difficult by varying the hitting among easy hits, hits to the left, and hits to the right. In all three cases, you will cause the fielder to play the ball, to go to the ball instead of only fielding those ground balls that come directly to him or her. You can make a game of it. Hit 10 grounders, 2 directly at the fielder, 3 to the left, 3 to the right, and 2 slow rollers. Keep score and allow 5 points for fielding the ball and 3 for blocking it.

CATCHING FLY BALLS

No skill will show more improvement with constant repetitive practice than catching fly balls. Starting with a tennis ball or rubber ball, have your child practice as described in Chapter 8 while you check the mechanics:

1. Eyes on the ball
2. Arms up and glove in position so ball will hit the pocket
3. Bare hand in position to cover the ball

COMBINATION DRILLS

If your child can recruit one or more teammates to practice with you, it will increase his or her level of interest and provide your child with some friendly competition in the preceding drills. Doing the following drills requires at least three kids at once.

Field, Throw, Catch, and Run Drill

This is a drill with four players at a time and a coach and is designed to simulate the most frequent play in baseball: fielding an infield ground ball. Players function as infielders (a second baseman and a first baseman), a runner, and a fielding pitcher. The coach hits ground balls to the infielder or pitcher, who fields them and throws to first base. The (helmeted) runner at home plate swings a bat at an imaginary ball on the tee. At the same time the coach, positioned up the foul line toward third base, hits the ball to the infielder. At the crack of the bat, the runner drops the bat and races to first base, running over it. Check the participant's performance on mechanics basics. Does the runner

- drop the bat (instead of throwing it)?
- run on the foul side of the first baseline to first base?

- run over first base without slowing down?
- touch first base with one foot as he or she runs over it?

Do the infielders

- get in set position?
- move to the ball (in and right or left)?
- keep body and butt low?
- keep eyes on the ball?
- "look" ball into the glove?
- use bare hand above glove in "alligator's mouth" hands position?
- take ball out of the glove as he or she pivots toward first?
- step toward first base as he or she releases the ball?
- throw accurately, to area of first baseman's head and chest?

Does the first baseman

- have proper foot touching the base?
- give infielder a target?
- catch ball in pocket while keeping the foot touching the base?
- bring bare hand over the ball to secure the catch?

Rotate the players to give them all some practice at each of the positions, which will add variety and interest to the drill.

"Hot Box" Drill

The "Hot Box" Drill, described in detail in Chapter 6, sharpens catching and throwing as well as running skills. It requires a minimum of three players, two basemen

The infielder keeps eyes on the ball and body low as he moves to meet the ball.

and a runner. With six players, you can run a second drill at the same time, without one interfering with the other—one drill between first and second base and the other drill between third base and home plate.

Basic Team Practice

The best team practice is to put a defensive team in the field and let the remaining players take turns batting and running the bases. Since it is practice don't let obvious mistakes go uncorrected, but be gentle in your criticism. Try to simulate game situations in which mistakes are commonly made to give the youngster who made the mistake enough chances until he or she can do it right. Then make the player feel good with praise and recognition of his or her accomplishment.

11
Being an Objective Parent

This is my third book on Little League Baseball and Softball. In each of the two previous books I felt parental perspective and decorum was important enough to devote a chapter to. The fact that I believe the subject requires still another chapter, in this book, may indicate that the situation has not improved.

Nearly every year you will read reports of lawsuits by parents against a coach, a league, or Little League, alleging discrimination against their children. There have also been documented cases of adults falsifying records of children on their teams in an illegal effort to win, including a celebrated case affecting the outcome of the 1992 Little League World Series.

In a review of my book *Managing Little League Baseball* in the *Chicago Tribune*, Robert Cross said, "*Little League* when used as a modifier for the word *parent,* has become . . . a synonym for abusive, overbearing, insensitive, or warped." Apparently the problem has existed since 1939, when Carl Stotz organized the first Little League in Williamsport, Pennsylvania. Mr. Stotz was motivated to remind parents in writing, "Little

League is for boys to have fun. Let's leave them alone to play the game."

Psychologist Thomas Tuko, author of the book *Winning Is Everything and Other American Myths*, calls youth sports a form of child abuse as approached by some parents. If you are a new parent to youth sports, I am sure you will be shocked by these indictments against Little League parents; if you are not new, you will be able to identify with these charges. Get any group of youth sports parents together, and they will have their own examples of the few abusive parents who threaten to spoil their children's sport. Fortunately there are enough parents who agree with President Bush's assessment of Little League Baseball. On its 50th anniversary in 1989, President Bush said "Little League is so special because it promotes ideals of sportsmanship, teamwork, citizenship, and a feeling of family—it is fathers and daughters, mothers and sons, together in a healthy arena."

The basic philosophy I have espoused in all three of my books, "Keep it simple; make it fun," will get *philosophical* nods of approval from parents, coaches, managers, umpires, and players. But often parents do not apply this philosophy in the "heat of battle": for example, when an umpire calls their child out on a close play; when an opposing manager gives an intentional walk to their child, who is a star player; when a coach constructively criticizes their child in practice; or when a team loses a close game to a better team. Some normally rational parents forget their objective philosophy and fail to "keep it simple; make it fun." The most amusing and ironic sight I recall seeing during my Little League experiences came after watching the end of a close game decided by an umpire's close, but obviously correct, call. It was a group of five adults—two managers, two other parents, and the umpire—shouting obscenities at each other at one end of the refreshment stand while their five children were sharing some refreshments at the other end, amused yet somewhat embarrassed by their parents' outrageous behavior! Two weeks later no one would even remember the score of the game, but at that moment it seemed to the parents like the most important issue in the world!

WHY DO PARENTS BEHAVE LIKE THAT?

Although I majored in psychology in college, I am not and never have been a practicing psychologist. I base my armchair psychological conclusions on 20-plus years of Little League observations as a parent, a coach, a manager, an umpire, and a League officer. During that time I have met some wonderful fellow parents, people who appreciated all of the good things that Little League and the Little League volunteers have done for their children. The others—the troublemakers who make Little League parent a bad name—are fortunately the minority. At a Little League officers' roundtable discussion, after each participant had told his favorite Little League parent story, we got serious and tried to determine how to spot the troublemakers and how to diminish the problem.

Spotting the Troublemakers

At our officers' discussion, we concluded that the reasons for the Little League parent problem are rooted in parent-child relationships that lack the level of objectivity that is needed. Examples of one-sided parental attitude are as follows:

- *Don't hurt my little child.* If their child cries, someone's to blame. If the child cries because the umpire called him or her out, the umpire's to blame. If it is because the child didn't play enough or was criticized, the manager's to blame.

- *My child is as good as any other player on the team.* Why doesn't he play as much as the others?

- *My child is better than any of the other players on the team.* Why doesn't the manager play my child more to help the team win?

- *The manager plays favorites.* And my child is not one of the manager's favorites.

- *My child doesn't do well because the manager puts too much pressure on her.* Doesn't the manager realize she is only seven years old?

- *The manager/coach criticizes my child.* I'm the only one who should do that. If the manager has a problem with my child, he should let me handle it.

- *I was a good baseball player; my child should be, too!* That coach doesn't know how to bring out the best in a player.

- *The other team's manager is [parents are or players are] ridiculing my child!* So I'll ridicule theirs, too. After all, turnabout is fair play.

The list could go on, but I think you get the picture.

How to Diminish the Problem

• *Develop a strong local board of directors for your league.* This is the group that sets the proper tone, enforces the rules, and deals with the troublemakers in your league. The key is to elect a majority of board members who are not active managers or coaches since it stretches objectivity to the limit when a manager or coach has to vote on an issue involving his or her team. In business they would call it a "conflict of interest."

The problem with implementing this recommendation is that good volunteers are hard to find, and sometimes the only volunteers will be parents whose children are currently active in the league. A local board should strive to elect at least a president who is strong and completely objective. And the president, in turn, should appoint strong, unbiased vice presidents of each league, Little League, Softball, Tee Ball, and so on, within the local organization. A local league with strong managing executives can be very effective at making playing in your league a positive experience for your child and the other children who participate.

• *Communicate with parents.* It is important to communicate the philosophy, rules, and enforcement provisions of your league. It is understandable that an uninformed parent attending his or her first Little League game might criticize the umpire and ridicule the other team, since that is what he or she might do at a major league baseball game.

Parents must bring their children to Little League registration, tryouts, and practice, so there are opportunities for face-to-face parent meetings. Indeed, attendance at an orientation meeting for parents could be made a condition of their child's acceptance to the program. At such a meeting, a frank discussion of the dos and don'ts for parents would be in order. Written communications to parents from both the league and from their children's managers should augment the orientation meeting. Samples of such league and manager letters were detailed in the chapter for parents in my book *Managing Little League Baseball.*

• *Screen managers and coaches.* Although a manager/coach will spend many hours with your child and has the opportunity to make a profound impression on him or her—good or bad—the only qualification a manager/coach must possess to get the position is the willingness to volunteer. In most cases, the volunteer is the parent of a child the same age as yours— which you would think would mean that the volunteer would be sensitive and responsive to your child or toward competitive sports and the other members of the team. This is not necessarily so, however, for the volunteer's attitude toward his or her own child or toward competitive sports may not be all you would desire in a manager or coach.

Interestingly, from my experience, managers and coaches are the easiest to recruit as volunteers. Umpires and refreshment-stand helpers are much more difficult to lure. Although prospective managers may not openly campaign, they are readily available, particularly as their children advance through each age level of competition. For example, Tee Ball League managers will want to manage their children's Minor League teams and Minor League managers will want to manage their children's Little League teams. And, as in many organizations, internal politics may determine who is appointed a manager by the league president. He has that authority mandated by national Little League regulations. That is why it is so important to have a strong, objective leader as your league president.

OBJECTIVITY/SUBJECTIVITY SCREENING OF PARENTS

I believe it would be appropriate to have volunteers— especially manager/coach volunteers—complete an application detailing experience and providing references from other parents whose children play with the volunteer's children. "Would you want this person to coach your child?" would be a good question to ask a reference in confidence. It could help a president make his choices for the all-important positions of team managers/coaches.

I have already made my disclaimer regarding being a psychologist, but, for what it's worth, I have developed the following 50-question, true-or-false test, which may be helpful in screening prospective managers and coaches for all levels of Little League. It simply measures their biases between the opposite scales of objectivity and subjectivity regarding their own children, their methods of motivating other children, and their attitude toward competitive sports for children. Even if you're not a volunteer, as an involved parent you should take and score the test yourself for your own information. Since the test measures a volunteer's point of view there are no right or wrong answers. However, the scoring of some questions is deliberately set up to identify patterns in attitude that would raise questions about the test taker's qualifications as a role model for children.

An Objectivity/Subjectivity Test for the Little League Parent

Circle either true or false, whichever better represents your own point of view.

1. I didn't push my child to play youth sports; it was entirely his [her] choice.   T   F

2. My spouse and I agree on whether or not our child should play in youth sports.   T   F

3. I have never had a disagreement with another parent about our respective children.   T   F

4. In competition, I have always been a good sport whether I won or lost.   T   F

5. I agree with Vince Lombardi's philosophy that "winning is everything." everything."   T   F

6. I could be objective as an umpire if my child were playing on one of the teams.   T   F

7. In Tee Ball, I think all players should   T   F
   play the same amount of time regardless
   of differences in age or ability.

8. Just because another player is better   T   F
   than my child doesn't justify letting that
   child play more.

9. If my child is better than another child,   T   F
   I think my child should play more, since
   it should help the team win.

10. If my child doesn't like sports, I   T   F
    shouldn't force him [her] to play.

11. Because I didn't have the opportunity   T   F
    to play organized sports, my child
    should play and appreciate the
    opportunity.

12. If it isn't important who wins, why keep   T   F
    score?

13. To gain a competitive edge, you have to   T   F
    teach the players that the other team is
    "the enemy."

14. If my child is better because I spend   T   F
    more time coaching him [her], the
    coach should recognize it and play my
    child more.

15. If I were a Little League coach and had   T   F
    to choose between keeping a good
    player in the lineup or substituting the
    good player with a poor player who
    hasn't had his [her] chance to play, I
    would be justified in keeping the good
    player in the lineup for the good of the
    team.

16. Managers and fans of major league
    teams berate umpires, so there is
    nothing wrong with my doing it at my
    child's games.   T   F

17. Rarely can an umpire's decision affect
    the outcome of a game.   T   F

18. If the same number of players on both
    teams have been called out on strikes, it
    means the umpire is being fair when he
    calls my child out on strikes.   T   F

19. Our manager, coaches, players, and
    fans should not ridicule the other team's
    manager, coaches, or players.   T   F

20. A manager should be held responsible
    for the negative actions of his players
    and their parents as well as his own.   T   F

21. I think a parent has an obligation to
    defend his or her child whether the
    child is right or wrong.   T   F

22. I believe "anything goes" if it helps
    your child's team win.   T   F

23. Parents should criticize their children
    when they play poorly, since it will
    make them better players.   T   F

24. I don't think any one of the managers
    in our league would cheat to help his or
    her team win.   T   F

25. I agree with Leo Durocher's saying that
    "nice guys always finish last."   T   F

26. A manager won't get the respect of his
    or her players and their parents unless
    the team wins.   T   F

27. If my child made every practice and   T   F
every game, he [she] should play more
than players who miss practice or
games.
28. Since a manager is a volunteer and puts   T   F
in a lot of hours for our children, he or
she should be allowed to manage the
team any way he or she wants to.
29. Managers should be allowed to   T   F
constructively criticize players on their
teams.
30. Parents should just cheer their child's   T   F
team and not jeer the other team or the
umpires.
31. Children have to learn to take criticism   T   F
and pressure because it will make them
better players.
32. I have a "low boiling point" and do get   T   F
in a lot of arguments.
33. I have been called a "hot head" on   T   F
occasion.
34. I agree with the adage "Spare the rod   T   F
and spoil the child."
35. I have never struck a loved one in anger.   T   F
36. I don't trust the other team's manager   T   F
or players, or even the umpire, because
they are out to beat my team.
37. My spouse or I have had one or more   T   F
disagreements with a teacher or the
principal at our child's school about the
handling of our child.

38. I would be justified in pulling my child out of a game if I thought the manager was treating him [her] unfairly.   T   F

39. I would be justified in criticizing an umpire if I thought he made a bad call against my child.   T   F

40. If my child cries when the umpire calls him [her] out on strikes, it is probably because the umpire is wrong.   T   F

41. I have trouble controlling my child.   T   F

42. My child will do anything I force him [her] to do.   T   F

43. My spouse doesn't approve of my behavior at our child's games.   T   F

44. I think the best players should play and the rest should ride the bench, the same as in school sports.   T   F

45. I believe in supporting my team's manager even when he [she] handles children poorly.   T   F

46. It doesn't bother me to hear our child's manager use profanity in front of the players.   T   F

47. I lose patience with my child frequently.   T   F

48. I was really good at sports, and with my help there is no reason why my child should not be at least as good as I was.   T   F

49. When you can't settle an argument verbally, you can always do it with your fists.   T   F

50. If I were a manager putting in a lot of volunteer hours, I would be justified in playing my child more than the other children on the team.   T   F

Objectivity/Subjectivity Test Scoring

Question Number	If Answered True	If Answered False
1	+1	−2
2	+1	−2
3	+1	−2
4	+1	−1
5	−2	+1
6	+1	−1
7	+1	−2
8	+1	−2
9	−2	+1
10	+1	−2
11	−2	+1
12	−2	+1
13	−2	+1
14	−2	+1
15	−1	+1
16	−1	+1
17	+1	−1
18	+1	−1
19	+1	−1
20	+1	−1
21	−2	+1
22	−2	+1
23	−2	+1
24	+1	−1
25	−2	+1
26	−1	+1
27	−1	+1
28	−1	+1
29	+1	−1

Question Number	If Answered True	If Answered False
30	+1	−1
31	−1	+1
32	−2	+1
33	−2	+1
34	−2	+1
35	+1	−2
36	−1	+1
37	−2	+1
38	−2	+1
39	−1	+1
40	−2	+1
41	−2	+1
42	−2	+1
43	−2	+1
44	−1	+1
45	−1	+1
46	−1	+1
47	−2	+1
48	−2	+1
49	−2	+1
50	−2	+1

Interpretation of Test Results

Arithmetically, there is a 140-point range between a high, positive score of +50 and a low, negative score of −90. The higher the score, the more objective the test-taker is likely to be about his or her child's participation in Little League; conversely, a low, negative score may indicate a self-serving attitude. A score at either extreme of the scale could indicate problems. For example, a very high scorer may be naive or has been untruthful in his or her answers. A very low score could indicate that the test-taker is too self-serving in the interest of his or her children or his team. Nevertheless, a reasonable, positive score should indicate an objective parent coach/manager, a volunteer who can work toward the goal to "keep it simple; make it fun."

IN CONCLUSION

In the introduction to this book, I expressed hope that the positive attitude I have witnessed among parents in Tee Ball will "percolate" into higher levels of Little League play. And I would like to end this book by echoing this fervent hope, in the best interest of our children.

Index